"Not only does Corey Miller offer practical tips on speaking with members of The Church of Jesus Christ of Latter-day Saints; he gives pertinent information regarding their theology in such a way that the Christian reader can't help but gain a better understanding and compassion for those imm........

Bill [barcode: D0807048] or, ry

"*Engaging with Mormons* ....lovingly sharing your faith with Mormon friends."

Sandra Tanner, Author; Founder, Utah Lighthouse Ministry (utlm.org)

"Corey Miller has that rare combination of academic understanding and personal experience which makes his contribution to this discussion invaluable. As someone who has been involved in campus ministry in Utah for over thirty years, I look forward to sharing this book with students and faculty alike!"

Rob Gunn, Cru staff, Utah/Idaho

"Corey Miller offers an accessible and practical book on the Mormon belief system. Here he provides helpful information for both discussing Mormonism and for sharing the gospel with Mormons. Coming from a former Mormon, this book provides you with a good overview of the Mormon faith and how it relates to Christianity."

Dr. Leo Percer, Associate Professor of Biblical Studies and Director of the PhD in Theology and Apologetics Program, Liberty University

"*Engaging with Mormons* is a helpful introduction to key concepts surrounding the history, doctrine, and worldview of Latter-day Saints. Corey has done an excellent job of articulating a winsome and practical way to engage LDS people. I love his tactics and illustrations! If you are looking to embody love while speaking the truth, then this is a great volume to help you start."

Dr. Bryan Hurlbutt, Lead Pastor, Lifeline Community, West Jordan, Utah; Author, *Tasty Jesus*; Contributor, *Sharing the Good News with Mormons*

"Dr. Corey Miller weaves together historical, cultural, and theological LDS thinking and experience in a time when, as for the last 30 years, so many facets of the Mormon world are changing under its leadership. This book will enlighten anyone wanting to be introduced to the subject of Mormonism in a balanced way."

Dave Roberts, Pastor, Church of the Risen Christ, Sandy, Utah

"Mormons are warm, gracious, non-Christian religious people. Dr. Corey Miller's story, expertise, and experience help tremendously in showing us how to engage with these people who so desperately need the real Jesus."

Bret Johnson, Former Pastor; President, The Hastening

"Instead of focusing on doctrinal disputing, Corey helps Christians get out of the weeds and into the minds of Mormons. As a pastor in Utah, I am grateful for this book."

Mike Bell, Pastor, South Mountain Community Church, Draper, Utah

ENGAGING
with...

Mormons

understanding their world
sharing good news

Corey Miller

thegoodbook
COMPANY

Engaging with Mormons
© Corey Miller, 2020

RATIO
CHRISTI
BOOKS

Published by:
The Good Book Company

thegoodbook
COMPANY

thegoodbook.com | www.thegoodbook.co.uk
thegoodbook.com.au | thegoodbook.co.nz | thegoodbook.co.in

Unless indicated, all Scripture references are taken from the Holy Bible, New International Version. Copyright © 2011 Biblica, Inc. Used by permission.

ISBN: 9781784984618
Design by The Good Book Company / ninefootone creative
Printed in the UK

Also in this series:
- Engaging with Hindus
- Engaging with Atheists
- Engaging with Muslims
- Engaging with Jewish People

Contents

This book is dedicated to several people on my journey. First and foremost, to my mother, Lynette Sopko, who sacrificially raised me with unconditional love. To my aunt, DeEtte McLachlan, who was the first to introduce me to the biblical concept of the gospel when I knew no other than that found in Mormonism. To Don, Mary, and Jeff Wallen who invited me, housed me, and provided the first context for me to be challenged to receive Christ in 1988. To Bret Johnson, my first youth pastor, who was seminal in my development by pouring into me that first year and later giving me my first opportunity in ministry. To Timothy Oliver, the former LDS missionary-turned-Christian, who helped straighten out my thinking early on when I left Mormonism to follow Christ. To Dave Roberts, my pastor in Utah, whose discipleship lifestyle is unmatched. Finally, to my in-laws, Bob and Lynnae Ness, who've lovingly absorbed me and my family into theirs through the gift of their daughter, Melinda, as one of the brightest spots in my life.

Corey Miller

Engaging with...

Preface

Christians have a wonderful message to tell the world. As the angel said at the birth of Jesus, it is "good news that will cause great joy *for all the people"* (Luke 2 v 10). But sometimes we have been slow to take that message of forgiveness and new life to others.

Sometimes it's because we have become *distracted.* There are so many things that can push the need to tell others from its central place in our calling as individuals and churches. We get wrapped up in our own church issues, problems and politics. Or we get sidetracked by the very real needs of our broken and hurting world, and expend our energies dealing with the symptoms rather than the cause.

Sometimes it's because we have lacked *conviction.* We look at people who seem relatively happy or settled in their own beliefs, and just don't think Jesus is for them. Or perhaps we have forgotten just how good the good news is, and how serious the consequences are for those who enter eternity unforgiven.

But often it has been *fear* that has held us back from sharing the good news about Jesus. When we meet people whose culture, background or beliefs are so different from ours, we can draw back from speaking about our own faith because we are afraid of saying the wrong thing, unintentionally offending them, or getting into an unhelpful argument that leads nowhere.

This little series of books is designed to help with this last issue. We want to encourage Christian believers and whole churches to focus on our primary task of sharing the good news with the whole world. Each title aims to equip you with the understanding you need, so that you can build meaningful friendships with others from different backgrounds, and share the good news in a relevant and clear way.

It is our prayer that this book will help you do that with Mormon people wherever you meet them: a neighbor, friend, work colleague, or missionary. We pray that the result would be "great joy" as they understand that the true message of Jesus is good news for them.

Tim Thornborough
Series Editor

Introduction

Why do Christians need a book about engaging with Mormons?

After all, Mormons are generally very nice people. And the official name of their church, The Church of Jesus Christ of Latter-day Saints (LDS), seems to center on Jesus. Surely, anyone who belongs to such a church is a Christian already?

But what if the LDS perspective is not simply another testimony about Jesus? Instead, what if it is a testimony about another Jesus? What if Mormons need to hear the true gospel just as urgently as anyone else?

That is the conviction of this book. Given that most of us don't know much about Mormon beliefs, plus our wider cultural reluctance to label any belief as "wrong," most Christians are often afraid, mystified, or otherwise apathetic to sharing their faith with Mormons, as if it does not really matter. It does matter! As we'll see later, it's a matter of life and death.

I love Mormons. Much of my family is Mormon, and has been for seven generations. We can trace our roots as far back as 1836, just six years after the Book of Mormon was published. I lived in Utah as a Mormon for the first 16 years of my life, and, after coming to Christ, lived there another three years as a Christian. I have experienced Mormon culture both as an insider and an outsider. I've also been a pastor and a professor of comparative religions at a university, and now work for a ministry that seeks to share the gospel on campus. And I can say this with certainty: God loves Mormons.

But because I love Mormons, I simply cannot love Mormonism. The latter threatens the former. So this is a book for any Christian who wants to lovingly engage Mormons with the truth—but who isn't sure where or how to start. It will help you talk compellingly and compassionately to Mormon friends, family, neighbors, colleagues, and missionaries.

Who are Mormons?

So, who are Mormons? As a matter of branding, they don't want you using the word "Mormonism" anymore.[1] According to the Church website, when describing the combination of doctrine, culture and lifestyle unique to the Church of Jesus Christ of Latter-day Saints, the term "the restored gospel of Jesus Christ" is preferred. While that may be preferred, the Bible-believing Christian won't grant that what Mormons have is the "restored gospel."[2] In this book we will continue to use "Mormonism" or "LDS," not out of disrespect, but simply due to those being the words in common use.

Mormonism is a religion with a great deal of affluence and influence. At the end of 2019, there were almost

70,000 full-time Mormon missionaries. Nearly every election cycle we see at least one Mormon running for the presidency of the United States. While only 2% of the US population is Mormon, they make up 6% of the US Senate. The LDS Church has more than 16 million members around the world, and is still growing (although not quite as quickly as it was a few years ago).[3]

Mormons are a people who are zealous for God, but whose zeal is not according to the knowledge of God. Mormons are very successful people, often contributing to societal good. They are a people with whom evangelical Christians share much in common, in terms of moral and political views. But we do not share the same theology—not even close. In view of our cultural and moral similarities and theological differences, one Christian seminary president said in his address to an audience of Mormon college students, "I do not believe that we will go to heaven together. But we may go to jail together."[4]

Bash or dash?

As we seek to engage with Mormons, there are two approaches that we need to avoid: I call these the "bash" and "dash" approaches.

The "bash" approach looks more like blasting opponents than it does blessing neighbors. Some people mock Mormons and look for every opportunity to "prove them wrong," merely to win an argument. Obviously, this is more likely to make enemies rather than converts. As in all evangelism, when engaging with Mormons the aim is to win the person rather than merely winning an argument.

Equally ineffective is the "dash" approach, which tries to avoid meaningful interaction. Perhaps we draw the blinds and close the curtains upon seeing the LDS missionaries approaching our door, pretending not to be home. Or if we do open the door, we simply tell the Mormon, "Thanks, but no thanks, I have my own religion," before quickly shutting it.

While slightly more polite, this attitude of disengagement or indifference is not going to result in Mormons coming to Christ. It may be that such Christians regard Mormonism as just another Christian denomination; or that they are wary of upsetting the relationship they have with a Mormon friend or colleague. But those who know Christ and want to make him known will resist an attitude of indifference or ignorance. Instead we'll seek to engage with gentleness and respect (1 Peter 3 v 15-16) and yet in truth and love (Ephesians 4 v 15).

This book will equip you to take a more fruitful approach than either "bash" or "dash." We won't spend much, if any, time explaining non-essential doctrinal aspects of the Mormon religion that you may have heard about (such as not drinking coffee, wearing special underwear, or symbols on the Temple). Instead we'll respectfully consider the Mormon essential theological beliefs that we need to know in order to effectively reach them in relatively simple and enjoyable conversation. We'll learn how to ask thought-provoking questions to stimulate critical thinking and to draw out ideas and underlying assumptions. We see this same approach employed by the apostle Paul and Jesus in their use of argument and questions. It requires that we know or learn something about our audience—including its core theology—for persuasive communication honoring to God.

All that said, if you're looking for ironclad rules of universal logic with which to combat false belief, you won't find them. For one thing, Mormons don't always use logic when it comes to religion. There is also a wide variety in Mormon belief and practice—find five different Mormons and you may get six different opinions (this includes LDS leaders).

Most people don't join the Mormon Church for intellectual or doctrinal reasons—often they have more emotional reasons, or the attraction of the security and community that the church offers. That isn't to say that we shouldn't use reason, but it is to say that we need to discover why a particular person is a Mormon: what attracts her to this and how deeply rooted is her commitment? We need to witness to a person as a whole person, being mindful of the fact that everyone that we meet brings to the conversation their own culture, personal history, and a complex web of fears, hopes, joys, and struggles. Sometimes an individual may need an argument or a reason to believe, but other times they may need a hug or a shoulder to cry on. It is imperative that we be prepared for this (1 Peter 3 v 15-16).

As one pastor and ex-Mormon in Utah put it, "When we limit our engagement with Mormonism to comparing truth claims, we ignore much of what matters to Mormons themselves."[5] So let's start by looking at Mormon culture.

Glossary of useful terms

Apostle: One of the LDS Church's 12 living apostles (Quorum of the Twelve Apostles) who govern the LDS Church under the president. When an apostle dies, another man is called to replace him.

Book of Mormon: One of the four books making up the Mormon scriptures. Joseph Smith claimed that he discovered the text of the Book of Mormon in 1827, written on gold plates, and subsequently translated it. It purports to tell the history of the ancient Americas and how Jesus established his church there.

Brigham Young: The second president of the LDS Church (1847-1877), and the founder of Salt Lake City. Brigham Young University (BYU) is named after him.

Celestial glory/celestial kingdom: The highest level of heaven in LDS theology. Mormons believe that after final judgment, people will be assigned to either the telestial, terrestrial or celestial kingdom. (Only a small number will be cast out to the "outer darkness" with Satan.)

Doctrine and Covenants (D&C): One of the four Mormon holy books, mainly containing beliefs and commandments that Mormons seek to abide by.

Great Apostasy: The belief that, after the time of Jesus' first apostles in the first century, there was a great falling-away; the true faith was lost and corrupted for centuries, until it was restored by Joseph Smith.

Heavenly Father: The title that Mormons use for the God who rules our world.

Joseph Smith: The founder and first president of the LDS Church (1805-1844).

Nephites and Lamanites: Two people groups that the Book of Mormon claims lived in the ancient Americas.

Pearl of Great Price: One of the four Mormon holy books, containing various teaching by Joseph Smith and writings purportedly by Abraham.

Prophet: Another title for the president of the LDS Church; believed to be God's spokesman on earth and exclusively able to receive authoritative revelation from him.

Sacred Grove: The place where Joseph Smith was said to have had his "First Vision" after praying about which church was right to join. Smith claimed that God told him that all the churches had become corrupt, but that he would provide a restoration plan through Joseph Smith. As such, this is a foundational event in Mormonism.

Saints: LDS believers.

Temple: A place of worship where Mormons perform special ceremonies and ordinances. The 160+ temples around the world are considered to be very sacred and only members of the Mormon Church can enter. Regular Sabbath worship takes place in meetinghouses/chapels, which are open to non-members.

Testimony: A Mormon person's sincere conviction that the key beliefs of Mormonism are true. It will usually include claims that Jesus is the Son of God and carried out the atonement; that Joseph Smith is a true prophet; that the LDS Church is the true church; and that its president is God's living prophet today.

Understanding Mormons

Chapter one

Understanding Mormon culture and values

Whether one comes into Mormonism by conversion or by upbringing, one quickly becomes immersed in a culture. From small insider nuances picked up in movies like *Napoleon Dynamite*, to church dances and expressions like "Oh my heck!", the cultural capital of Mormonism is about more than religious beliefs. Mormonism forms a way of life from cradle to grave. There are programs and community groups for all ages that are involved in shaping the Mormon identity.

Central to this community identity is a shared past. We'll think more about the roots of Mormonism in the next chapter. But for now, we'll note that central to the "Mormon story" are the Mormon pioneers who trekked westward to settle in Utah in the 1840s in a bid for religious freedom. These pioneers were led by Brigham Young (sometimes called "the Mormon Moses"). Today, part of the Mormon identity continues to include a sense of being a persecuted people, and an associated sense of solidarity. This "persecution complex" makes them fragile to criticism, with the voices of critics often providing a sense of validation to the Mormons as the persecuted people of God. So we must be careful in our witness lest we be perceived wrongly as anti-Mormon and simply reinforce their belief.

This shared Mormon history feeds into shared cultural practices in the present. I recall living outside of Utah and receiving a call from my mother who had planned to come visit me. She told me that she switched her dates from around July 24 to something else because she mistakenly thought that I would have plans celebrating that day. Why assume I had plans? Because she was thinking Utahn! On July 4, Americans celebrate Independence Day. On the July 24, Mormons will have a bigger firework display than on the Fourth, to celebrate Pioneer Day—commemorating the day Brigham Young arrived with the Mormon Pioneers to found Salt Lake City in 1847, declaring "this is the place."

Mormonism is not simply a cult; it is a culture. If you've ever spent significant time in Utah, this comes as no surprise. It is a state in America, but it is unique amongst all 49 others. Mormons have a somewhat distinct ethnic subculture within the broader American culture, and Utah Mormonism gets exported to Mormon communities everywhere. Cultural icons include:

- **The Temple and Temple Square:** This is the equivalent of the Vatican for Catholics or the Muslim worship center in Mecca. Every street address in Salt Lake is labelled relative to the Temple, a building which eclipses everything else downtown.

- **Brigham Young University (BYU):** BYU is owned by the LDS Church, has over 30,000 students enrolled, and is the largest private employer in Utah.
- **Genealogical Library:** The Family History Library is one of the biggest of its kind in the world, with over 2 billion names in its records. Its importance is tied to the Mormon doctrine of baptism for the dead and the belief that "families are forever" (more on this later).
- **Mormon Tabernacle Choir:** This is sometimes called the "Choir of the Presidents" since it has sung for every US President since William Taft. Their weekly broadcast, Music and the Spoken Word, is the longest-running network radio program in the world, and the choir has gold and platinum albums.

While these cultural institutions are all in Utah, they are all important for Mormons across the globe.

Another important part of Mormon culture are the various religious ceremonies which mark each stage of life. Babies are presented to the elders of the church to receive a baby blessing. Children are usually baptized and confirmed at age eight. (Converts become members via baptism and confirmation as well.) Children are often given CTR rings ("Choose the Right") to remember their commitments. I recall the sadness I felt when I lost mine. Male youth enter the priesthoods—Aaronic and Melchizedek—from the age of 12 and 18 respectively. Both males and females are encouraged to seek the "patriarchal blessing" of a priesthood leader, often as a teenager. This is a sort of personalized prophecy where one usually learns of which tribe of Israel they belong (usually Ephraim), along with receiving some promises for the future. Faithful Mormons are encouraged to serve on a self-funded, 18-24-month mission as a young adult. There are currently around 100,000 full- or part-time missionaries.

Core values
As well as these cultural practices, Mormon culture is also marked by a number of shared values.

1. Family
Mormons are very family-oriented, and big families are the norm for theological reasons. The LDS Church teaches that "families are forever"—that is, that Mormon families will stay together in eternity. This is central to the thinking of many people both in becoming LDS, and in remaining LDS. It is in families that people progress spiritually to the "celestial kingdom" beyond death. Family lineage is one reason that Mormons find genealogy so interesting. They care for their ancestors and want to conduct ordinances on their behalf. Family is so central to the entire theology and culture that one's attempt to convert a Mormon merely with rational argumentation sometimes falls on deaf ears.

I recall chatting with a young man inside the Visitors Center at Temple Square in Salt Lake City, Utah. It is rare to converse with a solitary Mormon missionary since they strategically travel in pairs. But in this case I had one isolated, and had taken him through my favored "methodology" for sharing the gospel with Mormons, which looks at the Book of Mormon's teaching on salvation (more on this in chapter 5). At the end, just when I thought I "had him," he replied, "If what you say is true would I have to leave the Mormon Church?" I said, "If what I'm saying is true then you'd want to leave just as I did, because it will take you to hell." He said, "Then I won't do it. I can't turn my back on my family." I was utterly shocked. I had him at the precipice, or so I thought… save one factor: family. If we are to understand this culture, we must see that family trumps truth for many Mormons.

That said, it's worth remembering that, according to the sociologist Rodney Stark, "at any given moment, the majority of the Latter-day Saints are first-generation converts."[6] This is important because it means that most Mormons, as first generationers, have the least invested in it. Anecdotal evidence provided by pastors I've spoken with in Utah shows that these new converts are the most likely to leave Mormonism, and that up to half of converts to Mormonism in the US leave after one year. But once they baptize kids and grandkids, it is harder for them to leave.

Others are reluctant to leave because of the broader sense of community that Mormonism provides. I have a dentist friend who no longer believes but who won't leave because of the community it provides for his kids and the clientele he stands to lose if he left.

2. Personal revelation

The idea of "personal revelation" is also highly valued among faithful LDS. Many discussions with LDS people result in their invoking this oft-cited passage from one of their holy books, the Doctrines and Covenants: "Behold, I say unto you, that you must study it out in your mind; then you must ask me if it be right, and if it is right I will cause that your bosom shall burn within you; therefore, you shall feel that it is right" (D&C 9:8). The "burning in the bosom"—something a Mormon deeply feels—confirms for him or her that Mormon teachings are true and valid, regardless the evidence. There are few things that a Mormon seeks more earnestly or treasures more highly than this experience, which is called his or her "testimony." This "personal testimony" is so powerful for the faithful Mormon, that it is a major aspect of their culture. Without a testimony you are not considered "in." Thus, the pressure to acquire one (or make one up) can be huge.

Because personal revelation is so important in Mormonism, LDS believers usually also have a high regard for the authority of the Mormon Church, its leaders and its teaching. The LDS Church is led by a president, who is also called "the prophet." As such, it is believed that the prophet is able to speak the word of God and establish doctrine.

What are we to make of this? The Bible is clear that God has revealed himself objectively through creation (Romans 1), the prophets (Matthew 5 v 17-19), and supremely through the Lord Jesus (Hebrews 1 v 1-2), and the Apostles who bore witness about him (Colossians 1 v 25). These sources give us all the truth that we need to believe for salvation and to live the Christian life (2 Timothy 3 v 16). So internal testimony must be consistent with the external testimony of the Bible.

As we seek to minister to Mormons, we must not underestimate the power of the feelings that these folks have experienced. We must also remember that any Mormon we are witnessing to must overcome the notion that the LDS Church authorities can never be wrong if they are ever going to make progress in a personal search for truth. One can imagine the difficulty in reading the Bible while always having the question in mind: "What do the LDS Church authorities think about this?"

One caveat to remember here is the fact that, just as there are many "tribes" of Christians—some of whom are antagonistic to tradition and church authority—so too there are many types of Mormons. Some Mormons can be found to "pick and choose" on doctrines (for instance, some Mormons take a liberal stance on things like homosexuality, and simply disregard scriptural teaching and are disgruntled about the official LDS stance).

There is hope!

Perhaps reading about the powerful cultural ties that bind our friends to Mormonism is making you doubt that they will ever leave. But don't despair. People can, and people do. Often it is in regard to these very areas that we find a "way in" for the gospel.

For instance, take the fact that the LDS person is expected to make sense of their religious experience by what they feel. Feelings are almost something synonymous with faith for Mormons—facts follow in the wagon, as it were. This means that many feel guilty for doubting, not to mention anticipating trouble ahead if their doubts are reported to others. It is not atypical for the first response to the doubts to be something like, "What's wrong with me? I must have a problem." Because Mormonism does not provide a natural framework for dealing with doubts and ambiguity, Christians have an opportunity to present a message that puts the "horse" of facts before the "cart" of feelings.

That said, most former Mormons who have converted to Christianity experience, at one time or another, a crisis of trust. They are required, as Mormons, to state from an early age that "The Church is true, and that Joseph Smith is a true Prophet of God." When the realization hits that this rehearsed and often repeated "testimony" is false, they become even more fearful of trusting a religious authority, which is why Christians need to be prepared to defend the historical trustworthiness of the Bible. Perhaps this crisis of trust is one of the greatest challenges for the Christian to overcome in their relationship with a Mormon friend.

Some disillusioned Mormons end up throwing the proverbial baby out with the bathwater and abandoning religion altogether. As one disaffected Mormon told me, "It's hard to be 'born again' because no one wants to be 'burned again.'" Having been lied to by one church, they don't want to be burned again.

But don't despair. While the odds are stacked against Mormons leaving the community, these factors are no match for the Spirit's power as we share the gospel of Christ and seek to live it out. In my own experience, part of what convinced me to embrace the real, biblical Jesus was seeing the love of Christ in a believing community on a Christian summer camp. I could see something different in that community that I had never seen before in Mormonism.

So love well, speak truth, and pray earnestly—and trust God's Spirit to do the rest.

Don't stereotype Mormons or assume you know what your LDS friend believes. You might be surprised. Sometimes you can ask five different Mormons and get six different answers!

Do ask questions. Listen and understand first; form your approach second. You have two ears and one mouth for a reason!

Don't expect every Mormon to be in the LDS Church because of doctrinal matters. Find out where your individual Mormon friend is at in terms of their awareness and attitude towards standard LDS teachings; what really motivates them?

Do invite them to a church or otherwise social event, your small group, your house, and so on. Bake them cookies and provide juice rather than coffee, please! (Official LDS teaching prohibits the consumption of caffeine or alcohol.)

Do get to know them on a first-name basis, even the missionaries who like to be called "Elder/Sister so-and-so," which is both dry and unbiblical. Ask them personal (albeit socially appropriate) questions.

Do show genuine appreciation for the "good" things in Mormon culture. It does wonders for building bridges rather than walls. It heightens their curiosity as to why you aren't LDS if there is so much you can appreciate about it. Love your Mormon friend and share the truth!

Chapter two
The Mormon story and scriptures

Like all cultures, Mormonism rests on a unique cultural story that shapes the way Mormons see themselves today. So buckle up and get ready for a whistle-stop tour of the history of Mormonism.

The "First Vision" of Joseph Smith (1820)

This is the founding story of Mormonism. For the Mormon, this is much the equivalent as Moses' encounter with God in the burning bush or Gautama Buddha attaining his "enlightenment" beneath the Bodhi tree. It centers around Mormonism's founder and first prophet: Joseph Smith.

Smith was born in Vermont in 1805. During his childhood there were many religious revivals taking place where he lived, with a number of different churches springing up. As the Mormons tell it, at the age of 14 Smith read a passage in the New Testament that inspired him to pray, asking God to show him which church to join. He went into the forest to pray, and as he did so, God and Jesus Christ appeared to him. He wrote later, "I saw a pillar of light exactly over my head, above the brightness of the sun, which descended gradually until it fell upon me." Within that light, he saw two persons. One spoke his name and pointed to the other, saying, "This is my beloved son. Hear him!" Smith claimed that the Lord told him not to join any of the existing churches, because they were all wrong.

LDS people refer to this incident as the "First Vision." It changed Smith forever, and would become central to the LDS claim that their Church is restoring Christ's true gospel to the earth.

Publication of the Book of Mormon (1830)

Mormons believe that Smith was led to a hill near Palmyra, New York, where he received an ancient record from an angel known as Moroni. Allegedly, engraved on gold plates was the history of a people who lived on the American continent during the time of Christ. It was from these plates that Smith is said to have translated the Book of Mormon. We'll come back to the contents of the Book of Mormon (and the problems with it) later in the chapter.

The Book of Mormon was published in 1830, and soon after Smith and his followers began meeting formally as "The Church of Christ."

Early persecutions (1838)

By 1838 Mormonism was centered in Missouri, where converts continued to settle. Tensions between Mormons and non-Mormons spiraled into a spate of violence between August and November—known as the 1838 Mormon War—which ended with the Governor of Missouri ordering the Mormons to leave the state or face death, and Smith being arrested and imprisoned. (He later escaped and moved, along with thousands of his followers, to Nauvoo, Illinois.)

These early incidences of violence—just one example of a repeated pattern as Mormons moved from state to state in the 1830s and 40s—left Mormons with the sense that they were a persecuted people. This in turn provided a validation of their claims to be the one true Church, since God promised that his church would be persecuted.

Death of Joseph Smith (1844)

In 1844 Smith was charged with treason and imprisoned in Carthage, Illinois, awaiting trial. While there an armed mob stormed the jail and shot Smith and his brother. The "martyrdom" of Joseph Smith was seen by his followers as confirming his status as a prophet, and has given energy to the LDS cause ever since.

The trek west (1847)

After Smith's death, Brigham Young became the Mormon Church's leader. When the authorities ordered the Mormons to leave Nauvoo, they began to move West, with most of them eventually settling in Utah. This movement of nearly 100,000 Mormon pioneers is equivalent to the

Jewish exodus out of Egypt and into the "promised land" of Canaan. The settlers founded Salt Lake City and other towns along the "Mormon Corridor" (which stretches westwards from Utah to eastern California, northwards to include much of Idaho, and southwards to parts of Colorado and Arizona). This uniquely Mormon "pioneer history" helps to create the sense that Latter-day Saints are Mormons first, Americans second.

Polygamy and its "abolition" (1890)

The widespread practice of polygamy among the early Mormons exacerbated tensions between the US government and the growing Mormon theocracy, which had a military 1/3 the size of the US Army (my ancestor served as a Colonel). It was on these grounds that Utah was originally denied statehood when it applied in 1862. In 1890 the Mormon Church finally capitulated by issuing a ban on polygamy.

Open priesthood (1978)

Since the 1840s, African Americans had been excluded from the Mormon priesthood. This ban was reversed by LDS leaders in 1978. While critics see this "prophecy" as an opportunistic response to the civil rights movement, from a Mormon perspective, this doctrinal u-turn only confirms that "the heavens are open" with respect to divine revelation. And because the prophets have divine authority within the Mormon Church, even if an individual disagrees with them, it is wrong to question the prophet, because their authority is unassailable.

The Mormon scriptures

Mormons do not altogether discount the Bible, but they do believe that they possess further revelations from God. As such, they claim to enjoy a unique connection with the divine which orthodox Christians do not.

Biggest of all of these additional holy books is the Book of Mormon. In 1830 Smith said that the Book of Mormon contained "the fulness of the gospel of Jesus Christ to the Gentiles and to the Jews also" (Doctrine & Covenants 20:9). In 1841 he wrote, "I told the brethren that the Book of Mormon was the most correct of any book on earth, and the keystone of our religion, and a man would get nearer to God by abiding by its precepts than by any other book" (*History of the Church*, 4:461).

By 2010 there were 150 million printed copies. It plays a primary role in Mormon evangelistic efforts. LDS missionaries encourage investigators to read and pray over the Book of Mormon in order to receive a sense from the Holy Ghost that it is, like the Bible, the word of God. (This practice is based on a statement toward the end of the Book of Mormon found in Moroni 10:4-5.) Given that the Book of Mormon's doctrines differ only in subtle ways from those of Christianity, Christians reading it might be given a more positive first impression of Mormonism than if they were introduced first to Smith's later evolved theology. If a person first accepts the Book of Mormon as the word of God, it is then a small step to, second, accepting Joseph Smith as a prophet of God and, third, the LDS Church as God's only true church. These three beliefs are what make up the standard LDS "testimony"—a sort of statement of faith.

Investigating the Book of Mormon

The Book of Mormon purports to tell the history and theology of various groups of people living on the American continent—particularly the "Nephites" and "Lamanites"—in around the first century. Unsurprisingly, though, the book's account is not backed up by any historical evidence. Moreover, there are several archeological finds which directly contradict its claims.

If you raise the lack of historicity of the Book of Mormon with an LDS person, you're likely to be told that "absence of evidence is not evidence of absence." That is, they admit that while there is scanty evidence, it doesn't mean that evidence won't one day be found.

However, there are several problems with this response.

First, it equates lack of evidence for specific elements in the text with lack of evidence for the whole story. It is the whole thing, not just specific details, which is unsubstantiated.

For example, we do not need to be able to provide archaeological evidence for each of the details of the Bible to show that its general historical framework is accurate, and that major locations and people groups mentioned in it were real. That's easily done. The problem of the Book of Mormon is that we cannot confirm any of its locations, figures, or people groups, despite the claim that it describes an entire civilization. Not even the LDS Church will commit to a specific regional location where all this is supposed to have taken place. One can, by contrast, take a trip to Israel and engage in excavation for just a few hours and find things that are millennia old. I once spent a whole week excavating in the Kidron Valley—it was like being in an archaeological gold mine! Upon seeing the Brigham Young University campus in Jerusalem (where students can spend a semester abroad), I couldn't help but wonder whether the students studying there were troubled by the difference between the historicity of the Bible and the unhistorical Book of Mormon.

Second, there is not just a *lack* of evidence for the Book of Mormon, but significant *contradictory* evidence. For example, the dominant view among Mormons is that the location of the civilizations it describes was in Mexico or thereabouts. But history tells us who lived there during that time, and they don't resemble Hebrew peoples and their beliefs as the Nephites allegedly did. Moreover, if the stories in the Book of Mormon took place there, why were the plates allegedly found near Joseph Smith's backyard in upstate New York? In 2006 the Introduction in the Book of Mormon was changed in view of DNA evidence that not only failed to support the Book of Mormon but contradicted it. Whereas it previously said that the Lamanites were the principal ancestors of the American Indians, it now says they were only *among* the ancestors.

Two great assumptions

So how does all this affect how we share the gospel with Mormons? Mormonism makes two fundamental historical assumptions that create both an obstacle and an opportunity for Christians seeking to witness to them.

First, Mormonism assumes that there was a "Great Apostasy" in the time of the early church—a complete falling away from the truth as it was originally revealed.

The idea is that although Jesus established his church in Palestine (and in the Americas), when the last of his apostles died, the priestly authority to act and speak for God was lost. Error crept into the church, and the true gospel was obscured. When Joseph Smith first prayed about which church he should join, he claimed that God told him that he was to join none of them, "for they were all wrong; and ... all their creeds were an abomination in his sight."[7] This is significant because, according to Smith himself "nothing less than a complete apostasy from the Christian religion would warrant the establishment of the Church of Jesus Christ of Latter-day Saints."[8]

Second, Mormonism assumes that what it possesses is the true gospel, which has been restored after the Great Apostasy. As one Mormon apostle, Bruce R. McConkie, wrote, "If it had not been for Joseph Smith and the restoration, there would be no salvation."[9] Joseph Fielding Smith, the tenth prophet and president of the LDS Church, went so far as to say, "[There is] no salvation without accepting Joseph Smith. If Joseph Smith was verily a prophet, and if he told the truth ... No man can reject that testimony without incurring the most dreadful consequences, for they cannot enter the kingdom of God."[10]

This claim may sound audacious; but it pales in comparison to Smith's own words about himself: "I have more to boast of than ever any man had. I am the only man that has ever been able to keep a whole church together since the days of Adam. A large majority of the whole have stood by me. Neither Paul, John, Peter, nor Jesus ever did it. I boast that no man ever did such a work as I. The followers of Jesus ran away from Him; but the Latter-day Saints never ran away from me yet."[11] This is reminiscent of a hymn about Smith that was sung in my Mormon church when I was a boy, titled, "Praise to the Man."

All this means that there is a steep burden of proof resting on our Mormon friend to show that for thousands of years, since the death of the last apostle, millions of bright Christian thinkers and committed believers have been misinformed, misled, or otherwise severely lacking in their faith and theology—and have not had the authority to act for God. I often begin a conversation with Mormons along these lines using this imaginary scenario:

> Suppose we were out in the wilderness together and I briefly journeyed off on my own. Returning, I inform you that I just encountered God. I saw Him! He spoke with me! Moreover, he told me that all allegedly Christian sects, including Mormonism, were apostate and in need of restoration.

Now, obviously, this follows Smith's story closely. I then ask:

> Would you believe me if I made the claim to have seen God, then asked for you and all other people to leave their religions, begin tithing to my restored movement, and follow me as leader?

The answer, if one is being honest, is clear: no. I then continue:

What seems more probable: one man's claim to have seen God literally, entailing this great historical loss; or that this one man himself was lost, with a view of God(s) and salvation seemingly foreign to the Bible? If my encounter in the forest sounds incredible, and you would not believe me, how is this different from committing yourself to the words of Smith now and asking me to do the same?

Moreover, Jesus himself guaranteed that there would never be a total apostasy, even if small scale apostasy is admitted elsewhere in the New Testament (1 Timothy 4 v 1). Jesus said:

> And I tell you that you are Peter, and on this rock I will build my church, and the gates of Hades will not overcome it. **Matthew 16 v 18**

The "gospel" according to Mormonism

So what is the "restored gospel" that has supposedly been revealed to Mormons? How is it different from the biblical gospel?

The orthodox Christian salvation story begins at creation. But the LDS story begins much earlier. Smith didn't believe that God created the universe out of nothing. Rather, God reorganized pre-existent and eternal matter. Humans are also believed to be without beginning, with God merely creating our spirit beings from earlier material essence.

The Mormon story of our destiny begins in this pre-mortal realm, "the first estate." Two plans emerged as to how to bring God's children to himself: that of Jesus and that of Lucifer. In the Mormon view they are spirit brothers along with the rest of us. The former offered to make it a free choice people could opt for; the latter insisted all would be saved, but there would be no choice in the matter. The former, with his emphasis on free agency, won. Lucifer and his ilk were cast from heaven and became demons.

According to Mormonism, Jesus' plan required humans to be given mortal bodies on earth for a time of testing, which is our "second estate." This is an opportunity to be put on a path for eventual exaltation. Everyone will have a chance, in this life or the next, to hear the gospel and be able to respond accordingly. While some—very few it seems—will be cast into outer darkness, the majority will go to one of three degrees of glory in heaven: telestial, terrestrial, or celestial. The ultimate goal is the "celestial kingdom," where one can eventually become a god oneself, and the cycle starts over again, worlds without end.

We'll think more in chapters 4 and 5 about the differences between the Mormon view of salvation and what the Bible reveals. For now, note the Mormon emphasis on personal worthiness in order to achieve the ultimate goal. As LDS apostle Bruce R. McConkie wrote:

Man's purpose in life is to learn the nature and kind of being that God is, and then, by conformity to his laws and ordinances, to progress to that high state of exaltation wherein man becomes perfect as the Father is perfect.[12]

Other authorities in Mormonism

While the Book of Mormon is highly significant in Mormonism, it is not the only authority informing their beliefs and practice. Authoritative beliefs are derived from three major areas: the scriptures, the prophets, and the testimony.

The scriptures are made up of the four "standard works":

- **The Book of Mormon** (a history of the ancient Americas and how Jesus came and established his church among those who resided there).
- **The Doctrine and Covenants** (modern revelations, mostly of Joseph Smith, and only one of which was added last century).
- **The Pearl of Great Price** (books believed to have been written by Abraham and Moses as well as an official account of Smith's early prophetic work).
- **The King James Version of the Bible** (albeit in a corrupted and incomplete state).

The "prophets" are the former leaders/presidents of the LDS Church, beginning with Joseph Smith. While the living prophet takes precedence over his (dead) predecessors, all the words of the prophets are considered to be authoritative, as are official Mormon Church publications.

Last, but not least, is the personal testimony. Mormons place much stock in personal revelation. We'll return to this in the next chapter.

The existence of all these competing authorities means that landing on a systemized theology becomes difficult—both for the Mormon, and for the Christian trying to engage them! The former department head of philosophy at BYU, James Faulconer, said:

> For a Latter-day Saint, a theology is always in danger of becoming meaningless because it can always be undone by new revelation. ... [In] speaking for God, [the Prophet] can revoke any particular belief or practice at any moment, or he can institute a new one, and he can do those things with no concern for how to make his pronouncement rationally coherent with previous pronouncements or practices.[13]

Bible-loving Christians, however, can rejoice that we have God's full and final revelation to us in his word, that will not change. It is a firm foundation on which to build our lives, and on which to invite others to do the same. "The grass withers and the flowers fall, but the word of our God endures forever" (Isaiah 40 v 8).

Engaging with Mormons

Chapter three

Connecting through testimony

"I bear you my testimony. I know Joseph Smith is a prophet of God! I know the Book of Mormon is the word of God. And I know that the Church of Jesus Christ of Latter-day Saints is the one true church!"

Anyone who has talked for long with Mormon missionaries is likely to have heard a version of this little speech, which is referred to simply as "the testimony." It's often followed by a challenge to the "investigator" to pray sincerely and ask God to likewise give you a testimonial knowledge of the truth of Mormonism (based on a promise made in Moroni 10:4).

The testimony is often delivered with such expressive tenacity that one might be tempted to conflate it with truth. At the very least, Christians are usually perplexed about how to respond.

Far too many Christians walk away from spiritual conversations with Mormons, deflated by the fact that Mormons seem unreceptive to all the great facts and logical arguments Christians use and instead insist on clinging to their testimony. But facts don't always change minds. Instead, we need our Mormon friend to first begin to doubt their testimony before they can believe what we share. The best way to do this is through imaginative illustration and asking questions. After subtly creating a place of doubt, we can make use of their high esteem for testimonial knowledge by deploying our own personal testimony in conjunction with the powerful objective testimony of the Bible.

Four things to remember up front
Let's think a little more about testimony in general, before laying out a strategic approach to "the testimony" when sharing the gospel with Mormons. Here are four things to remember up front:

1. While the Mormon approach to testimony is problematic, we need not discount the value of personal testimony as a legitimate form of knowledge. There is both biblical precedent for, and rhetorical power in, sharing our own Christian testimonies.
2. We should initially commend (rather than attack or dismiss) the LDS person's bearing of their testimony as a means of locating common ground. We can say something like, "I can see that you hold those beliefs very sincerely," or "Thank you for sharing that with me." Mentioning agreement before disagreement

helps our Mormon friend to feel receptive rather than defensive.

3. We should aim to use questions and answers—rather than direct frontal assault—to engage, assess, and ultimately bring about doubt in the Mormon's testimony. Asking thought-provoking questions helps foster reflection rather than deflection. People are often better persuaded when they arrive at conclusions on their own than when they are pointed to them by others. Most active LDS members see themselves as having the repository of religious truth. Many are former missionaries and are used to being in the role of a teacher in conversations about their faith. Let them think they are "teaching" by asking them questions, and then lead them to the truth.

4. Remember that, given the influence the LDS testimony has, we will make little progress in discussing other essential matters such as God and salvation if we do not first undermine confidence in their testimony.

What the Bible says about testimony

Scripture is filled with passages that speak positively about the value of testimony where properly used. God's Spirit "testifies with our spirit that we are God's children" (Romans 8 v 16). In 1 John 5 v 9-13 the testimony of our assurance of eternal life is denoted as some sort of knowledge. Jesus says that eternal life consists in *knowing* God (John 17 v 3). Given the Holy Spirit in the life of the New Testament believer (John 14 – 16), one is expected to know experientially—not merely intellectually—that God is present in, and independent from, the world he created. So as a Christian, it's good to feel that your faith is true, and it can be powerful to talk about your experience to others.

The intuitive problem many people have with testimony as a form of knowledge is that it seems so subjective by nature. Plus, if I have a testimony, and you have a different testimony, then don't they cancel each other out? How can we possibly know what is true in the face of conflicting "evidence"? The problem with this objection, however, is that not all evidence is equal. Evidence needs to be weighed rather than counted: the subjective evidence of my testimony needs to be weighed against the objective revelation of God's word. If a person's beliefs involve contradictions with other known truths, then they would be false. Therefore, only testimonial reports that contradict truth or fail to be supportable by evidence are problematic.

Understanding the Mormon testimony

Christians are sometimes baffled after presenting what they take to be knock-down arguments against Mormonism, only to hear the Mormon double down about how they know it is true regardless, as if they are saying, "Never mind the facts; I've got a feeling." Although the prophets and scriptures are authoritative in Mormonism, it is usually the testimony that proves to be most influential on the average Mormon. LDS people aspire to "bear testimony" (that is, a personalized, deeply felt, public declaration). They deploy it in defense when cornered, or on offense to impact an investigator.

A selection of quotes from LDS writers might help you get your head around the Mormon understanding of the testimony. LDS apostle Boyd K. Packer said, "A testimony is to be found in the bearing of it. Somewhere in your quest for spiritual knowledge, there is that 'leap of faith,' as the philosophers call it."[14] Elsewhere, Packer reveals the nature of testimony: "Bear testimony of the things that you hope are true, as an act of faith."[15]

The Doctrines & Covenants 9:8-9 describe the testimony as a "burning in the bosom," which LDS apostle Dallin Oaks defined as "a feeling of comfort and serenity."[16] Another LDS leader encourages its use in evangelism: "Sincere feelings conveyed from heart to heart by means of testimony convert people to the truth where weak, wishy-washy, argumentative statements will not."[17] An official LDS Church manual proclaims, "In order to know that the Book of Mormon is true, a person must read, ponder, and pray about it. The honest seeker of truth will soon come to feel that the Book of Mormon is the word of God."[18] Another LDS apostle-turned-prophet even warned that the failure to bear testimony frequently may result in a loss of merit points toward the heavenly goal.

It seems as though the more expressively the testimony is told, the truer it becomes. Apparently, it is impenetrable to argument. It is that powerful!

Making room for truth

Given the stranglehold that testimony has on Mormons, it's important to undermine confidence in it in order to open new possibilities. How do we do that?

I find it helpful to use a "police lineup" illustration. In a police lineup, the suspect of a crime stands side-by-side along with several foils—people of similar height, build, and complexion—facing the direction of the witness who is behind a one-way mirror. The witness must identify the real culprit in contrast to the mere look-a-likes, who are eliminated in the process. I'll say something like this to my Mormon friend:

> So, we are trying to consider the testimony of Mormonism, which claims to be the true representation of God. But which Mormonism? There are numerous competing sects to line up and examine, all of whose testimonies disagree. Only one can be right.

Although Mormonism may look like a very uniform religion to the outsider, there are actually dozens and dozens of Mormon splinter groups. The Salt Lake City-based LDS Church is usually the one people think of when hearing the term "Mormon." But it is not alone. Most Mormons know this, even if they are unaware of quite how many competing sects exist. Each one is fully loaded with their own prophets and apostles claiming to hold the true "Restoration," which excludes all others. Furthermore, they all claim that they have received a testimony about the truthfulness of the Book of Mormon and their authorized and restored version of Mormonism, attended with great feelings of warmth and serenity.

On venturing in this direction, the Mormon may sense a familiarity with the LDS "origin story," when Joseph Smith went into the "Sacred Grove" to ask God which of the different Protestant churches to join. Many LDS missionaries will recount this story to people in their first missionary discussion. They often note that the multi-plicity of church denominations existing today is confus-ing. So, they argue, we need modern revelation through a living prophet to guide us through the confusion.

The police lineup illustration turns the tables so that it is the Mormon who is in the "Grove," so to speak, as we point out to them the diversity of their own movement and question the reliability of their testimonies. It is rhe-torically powerful because we are using "Mormonese"—the language of experience—and subverting their misuse of testimony while preparing to use our own testimony properly. (A Christian's testimony is likewise subjective but corresponds to the objective testimony of Scripture, which is historically reliable.) Remember, the goal is to undermine our Mormon friend's confidence in their sub-jective testimony so that every time they ponder bearing it going forward, with or without you present, they will be unable to feel confident given the residue of doubt. They will be more open to consider other things.

Here's another way to illustrate the problem with sub-jective testimony. Suppose that you want to inquire as to which of the Mormon sects you should join. You need only name a few. The Church of Jesus Christ of Latter-day Saints (LDS) is the biggest one; others include the Fundamentalist Church of Jesus Christ of Latter-day Saints (FLDS) and the Apostolic United Brethren (AUB). Ask your friend to imagine that you gather one repre-sentative from each in a room to bear you his testimony. Whether lining up four or five or fifty representatives, they all sincerely bear testimony and yet they all contra-dict each other at serious points—not to mention that each thinks the other to be apostate. The Sacred Grove is recollected once again.

How might an investigator conclude which of all these Mormon sects is true? Logically, since each one contradicts the others, at best only one can be true and all others false. At worst, they are all false. Invoking imagination via illustration again, one could ask:

Suppose I was standing before a lineup of various sects of Mormons, each with their own set of prophets and apostles bearing testimony. How would I determine which is true? How do you know your church is true and not another? As I see it, you have a few options. Either you can judge their hearts as liars or insincere people, or you can claim that, while sincere, they are somehow deceived by a lying spirit. Which do you opt for, given that you must assume your own testimony is true: that the other people are insincerely lying or sincerely deceived?

Get a commitment. Likely, given our cultural aversion to making judgments about people, they will choose the latter. Continue probing the issue, asking:

How do you know that it is not you who are sincerely deceived in your testimony? The apostle Paul warns that it's possible to be deceived by Satan masquerading as an angel (for example, 2 Corinthians 11 v 14, Galatians 1 v 6-9). How do you know that you are not the one who is deceived, when competing Mormon sects testify of an equally strong feeling of peace and serenity? It seems to me that a subjective testimony cannot be relied on as the sole criterion by which we determine what is true. Furthermore, if Mormonism teaches a different God or means of salvation which contradicts the Bible, then biblical Christians should no more pray about this than pray about whether we ought to murder—God has already spoken. So while knowledge of God can be transmitted via testimony, it is not wise to rely on subjective testimony as automatically meaning that something is true—especially if our eternity hangs in the balance. Would you agree?

Sharing Christian testimony

If the conversation gets this far, a gospel presentation is in order. Aim to communicate the essentials about God (he is the Creator of everything, is holy and worthy of our worship); man (we are sinful, have rejected God's authority, and are deserving of his wrath); Christ (he is fully God and fully man; he died on the cross to take the punishment his people deserve and rose again to offer us eternal life); and our response (to be saved we must repent of our sin and trust in Christ, and receive his free gift of forgiveness).

Having undermined my Mormon friend's testimony and shared the gospel, I'll then conclude by deploying my testimony and the most explicit statement in Scripture testing the legitimacy of a testimony, 1 John 5 v 9-13. Speaking with tenacity, I'll say, "I testify that in Jesus

Christ, and him alone, I have eternal life and will be with Heavenly Father for eternity. I'd like to share Scripture that explicitly details a true testimony that is divinely approved knowledge." I'll then take them to the words of Scripture:

> We accept human testimony, but God's testimony is greater because it is the testimony of God, which he has given about his Son. Whoever believes in the Son of God accepts this testimony. Whoever does not believe God has made him out to be a liar, because they have not believed the testimony God has given about his Son. And this is the testimony: God has given us eternal life, and this life is in his Son. Whoever has the Son has life; whoever does not have the Son of God does not have life. I write these things to you who believe in the name of the Son of God so that you may know that you have eternal life. **1 John 5 v 9-13**

I then inquire, "Do you have this testimony? If you died today, do you know that you would experience eternal life with Heavenly Father?[19] If not, is God a liar? I know that I have eternal life because I trust in Christ's work alone, doing good works in grateful response to the salvation I have solely on the merits of Christ. I know this by the Spirit and the testimony of Scripture. Mormonism does not offer the confidence that my testimony has, nor is it in harmony with God's testimony. He says that whoever 'has the Son' can know that eternal life with their Heavenly Father is assured." What a wonderful promise to hold on to and hold out to others!

Do express truth in love. We ought to love the Mormon while not loving Mormonism. And we ought to love the Mormon enough to tell them the truth. We can tell the truth without love, but we cannot love without telling the truth.

Do seek to be perceived as a truth seeker, because, well, we ought to be truth seekers! The Mormon, especially the LDS missionary, won't even continue the conversation for very long unless they perceive you as a truth seeker to whom they think they can successfully impart "truth."

Do remember that since the majority of adult Mormons have served a church mission, they are used to being in the "driver's seat" and teaching. Use questions to control the direction of the conversation while making them think they are teaching. In the words of author Jay Heinrichs, practice using "rhetorical jujitsu" by using your opponent's own moves to throw him off balance.

Don't get distracted from the essentials. Once you have unsettled the testimony, try to keep coming back to the doctrines of God, Christ, and salvation.

Do remember that Mormons are heart people. The ancient Greek philosopher Aristotle taught about three elements of the art of persuasion: logic (good arguments), ethics (the credibility of the speaker), and emotion. We often default to focusing on the first one, but when engaging with Mormons it is especially important to make the emotional connection.

Chapter four

Salvation, part 1: The performance trap

What must we do to be saved? A person's eternal future hangs on the answer to that question. And it is a question to which Bible-believing Christians will give a very different answer than the Mormon Church.

Like many Mormons, I grew up feeling overwhelmed with the prospect of reaching the highest glory of heaven. I knew I could try, but I was unsure whether my performance would be enough. Mormonism teaches that the process toward the good life involves two steps: salvation and exaltation. Salvation is understood in different ways. In a general sense, all people will be resurrected from the dead and live forever. But Mormonism also teaches that personal salvation is up to the individual. In order to acquire ultimate happiness after we die—exaltation in "celestial glory"—we must first achieve moral perfection. In this chapter we'll see that Mormonism does not present us with the true gospel but a false one—and how that places an unimaginable weight on people.

Bearing a heavy load on Mount Burden

When a Mormon is asked what is required for salvation, the typical LDS response is something like: "Faith, repentance, baptism, and receiving the Holy Spirit." Or more simply, in the words of a motto that I learned as a child, "Try, try your best, and God will make up the rest."

It is true that Mormons believe that salvation requires grace—a free and undeserved gift from God. BYU professor Stephen Robinson passionately claims:

> One sometimes hears that Latter-day Saints are not Christians because all true Christians believe in salvation by grace, while the Mormon believes in salvation by works ... This idea of salvation by works ... has nothing to do with LDS doctrine ... The charge that this is what Latter-day Saints believe badly misrepresents the LDS position.[20]

To be sure, grace is a big part of the process. Jesus' work in the atonement is essential for Mormons. He goes on to clarify:

> The fundamental LDS belief regarding grace and works is well within the spectrum of traditional Christianity ... The Latter-day Saints have never believed in salvation by any other means—and

especially not by individual works ... The LDS scriptures are clear—we are saved by grace.[21]

Robinson makes it very clear that the LDS faith teaches salvation by grace. The question is, though, do you need grace and something else? Consider this claim by an LDS apostle and prophet Spencer W. Kimball, who was the Mormon Church's president in the 1970s and 80s: "One of the most fallacious doctrines originated by Satan and propounded by man is that man is saved alone by the grace of God; that belief in Jesus Christ alone is all that is needed for salvation."[22]

The battle cry of the Protestant Reformation—a 16th-century movement away from the Roman Catholic Church toward a more biblical Christianity—was "By grace alone through faith alone." Men like John Calvin and Martin Luther taught that salvation is entirely a gift of God's grace—his unmerited favor. There is nothing we *can* do to earn it; and there is nothing we *need* to do to earn it. We simply receive it by faith. Hopefully, that idea is both familiar and wonderfully precious to you.

So what does Mormonism teach instead, if it's not "grace alone"? Another LDS apostle Boyd K. Packer beautifully illustrates this for us:

Let me tell you a story—a parable. There once was a man who wanted something very much. It seemed more important than anything else in his life. In order for him to have his desire, he incurred a great debt. He had been warned about going into that much debt, and particularly about his creditor.

But it seemed so important for him to do what he wanted to and to have what he wanted right now. He was sure he could pay for it later. So he signed a contract. He would pay it off some time along the way. He didn't worry too much about it, for the due date seemed such a long time away. He had what he wanted now, and that was what seemed important. The creditor was always somewhere in the back of his mind, and he made token payments now and again, thinking somehow that the day of reckoning really would never come. But as it always does, the day came, and the contract fell due. The debt had not been fully paid. His creditor appeared and demanded payment in full ...

The debtor had a friend (Jesus Christ). He came to help. He knew the debtor well ... he wanted to help because he loved him. He stepped between them, faced the creditor, and made this offer. "I will pay the debt if you will free the debtor from his contract so that he may keep his possessions and not go to prison." As the creditor was pondering the offer, the mediator added, "You demanded justice. Though he cannot pay you, I will do so. You have been justly dealt with and can ask no more. It would not be just." And so the creditor agreed. The mediator turned then to the debtor, "If I pay your debt, will you accept me as your creditor?" "Oh yes, yes," cried the debtor. "You saved me from prison and showed mercy to me." "Then," said the bene-factor, "you will pay the debt to me and I will set the terms. It will not be easy, but it will be possible. I will provide a way. You need not go to prison."[23]

I appreciate Packer's instinct to use a parable. Jesus taught in parables. The problem is that this parable clearly contradicts Jesus' teachings and the whole New Testament! In this parable, the person who owes the debt—the sinner—does not get his debt paid, cancelled, or otherwise forgiven. Rather, it seems more like his debt has been refinanced or simply transferred so that the debtor owes another creditor. People may transfer their mortgage from bank to bank, but the only time the householder comes to own the home is when the final payment is made. The deed finally arrives in the mail with these glorious words: *Paid in full.*

And "paid in full," according to the true gospel, is what Jesus cried from the cross when he declared, "It is finished" (John 19 v 30). His death in our place means that our sins are paid for—in full, finally, and forever. "It is finished" means there is nothing more for us to do. All we have to do is accept this free gift by faith.

The extreme performance mentality

Yet that is a very different offer than the one made by the Mormon "gospel." The standard LDS book of doctrinal instruction, *Gospel Principles*, has this to say:

Without Jesus Christ, who is our Savior and Mediator, we would all pay for our sins, which are our spiritual debts, by suffering spiritual death. But because of him, if we will keep his terms, which are to repent and keep his commandments, we may return to live with our Heavenly Father.[24]

The true gospel is that Christ paid the debt he did not owe because we owed a debt we could not pay. But Mormonism teaches that we still have a heavy debt to bear. Notice that conditional little clause: "if we will keep his terms."

All mortgages come with terms of agreement that two parties enter into when they sign the contract. Mormonism claims that God's terms, in order to live with him as our Heavenly Father, are for us to repent and keep his commandments. Often, people do not read the fine print in the contract—yet with eternity at stake it's important we understand exactly what these terms mean!

So what does it mean to "repent," in the Mormon view? Consider this, also from *Gospel Principles*:

> Repentance means not only to convict yourselves of the horror of the sin, but to confess it, abandon it, and restore to all who have been damaged to the total extent possible; *then spend the balance of your lives trying to live the commandments of the Lord so that he can eventually pardon you and cleanse you.* (Emphasis mine)[25]

By this reckoning, repentance seems to involve horror of sin, confession, abandonment, and even some restoration; it is also beholden on you to keep God's commandments going forward, so that God can pardon and cleanse your past (that is, forgive or pay the debt otherwise owed). Far from clearing the balance sheet, Mormonism teaches that repeated sins have the added burden of bringing back the debt of past sins and adding them back onto the principal balance owed.

This is a far cry from Jesus' offer of salvation to the thief on the cross: "Truly I tell you, today you will be with me in paradise" (Luke 23 v 43). It's true that the New Testament speaks of "the obedience that comes from faith" (Romans 1 v 5). True repentance will result in changed lives. But the New Testament teaches that we obey because we've been forgiven; we're not forgiven because we obey. That order is crucial.

If we get it the wrong way round, as Mormonism has, then this is a heavy burden to bear. This is profoundly depicted in Stephen Robinson's book *Believing Christ*, where he describes the experience of his wife, Janet. One night she explodes:

All right. Do you want to know what's wrong? I'll tell you what's wrong—I can't do it anymore. I can't lift it. My load is just too heavy. I can't do all the things I'm supposed to. I can't get up at 5:30, and bake bread, and sew clothes, and help the kids with their homework, and do my own homework, and make their lunches, and do the housework, and do my Relief Society stuff, and have Scripture study, and do my genealogy, and write my congressman, and go to PTA meetings, and get our year's [food] supply organized, and go to my stake meetings, and write the missionaries...[26]

Robinson remarks, "She just started naming, one after the other, all the things she couldn't do or couldn't do perfectly—all the individual bricks that had been laid on her back in the name of perfection until they had crushed the light out of her." But it did not stop there. Janet continues:

> No matter how hard I try to love everyone, I fail. I don't have the talent Sister X has, and I'm just not as sweet as Sister Y. Steve, I'm just not perfect—I'm never going to be perfect, and I just can't pretend anymore that I am. I've finally admitted to myself that I can't make it to the celestial kingdom, so why should I break my back trying?

It's very rare for a Mormon to express a sentiment like this. Yet the social pressure produced by LDS doctrine is overwhelming. Sometimes that manifests itself in more secretive ways. Maybe this is the reason why Utah is among the top consumers of anti-depressants like Prozac and Zoloft, often known as "stress drugs."[27]

Finally, Robinson writes:

> I asked Janet, "Do you have a testimony?" She responded, "Of course I do—that's what's so terrible. I know the gospel is true, I just can't live up to it." I asked her if she had kept her baptismal covenants, and she replied, "No. I've tried and I've tried, but I can't keep all the commandments all the time." I asked her if she had kept the covenants she had made in the temple, and again she said, "I try, but

no matter how hard I try, I don't seem to be able to do all that's asked of me."

Janet, the wife of a famous BYU professor, understands the gospel to mean something that she cannot live up to. It seems to be mission impossible. How can that be, when the word "gospel" itself means "good news"?

Yet if one's understanding is that salvation is by grace, through faith, plus an enormous load of works involved in the terms of the contract, then you end up feeling burdened and miserable. Worse than that, you end up outside of God's salvation: "All who rely on the works of the law are under a curse ... No one who relies on the law is justified before God, because 'the righteous will live by faith'" (Galatians 3 v 10-11).

The "miracle" of earned grace

Let's think some more about the Mormon teaching that true repentance does not permit making the same mistake again. That was the view put forward by Spencer W. Kimball in his book, *The Miracle of Forgiveness*:

> Repentance must involve an all-out, total surrender to the program of the Lord. That transgressor is not fully repentant who neglects his tithing, misses his meetings, breaks the Sabbath, fails in his family prayers, does not sustain the authorities of the Church, breaks the Word of Wisdom, does not love the Lord nor his fellow men ... God cannot forgive unless the transgressor shows a true repentance which spreads to *all* areas of his life.[28]

Furthermore, Kimball speaks of…

> the repentance that *merits* forgiveness. It is that the former transgressor must have reached a "point of no return" to sin wherein there is not merely a renunciation but also a deep abhorrence of the sin—where the sin becomes most distasteful to him and where the desire or urge to sin is cleared out of his life.[29]

Now let us pause for a moment. Kimball was not a mere BYU professor or Mormon bishop. He went on to be none other than the president and apostle—a position which classed him as God's mouthpiece to the LDS Church and the world, the interpreter of scripture and the officiator of proper LDS thought on important matters.

Kimball makes clear that all former sins—all former payments made on the mortgage—return if one does not reach moral perfection:

> To return to sin is most destructive to the morale of the individual and gives Satan another hand-hold on his victim. Those who feel that they can sin and be forgiven and then return to sin and be forgiven again and again must straighten out their thinking. Each previously forgiven sin is added to the new one and the whole gets to be a heavy load.[30]

This idea that one's forgiveness can be cancelled if one reverts to sin stems from Doctrine and Covenants 82:7

which states, "unto that soul who sinneth shall the former sins return."

In the Mormon view, the commandments can be viewed as rungs on the ladder placed down into a pit to enable us to climb out one step at a time. As each step is made, one advances closer and closer toward the top of the pit, where grace exists to cover one's past upon arrival. But grace is not granted, one is not secure, until one is finally and fully out of the pit. For any sin—any at all (including drinking a Starbucks coffee, which is prohibited by the "Word of Wisdom" mentioned in the quote above)—will bring about a fall all the way back down to the bottom of the pit to start all over again as though one were signing a 30-year mortgage for the very first time. As Kimball forcefully concludes:

> Eternal life hangs in the balance awaiting the works of men. This progress toward eternal life is a matter of achieving perfection. Living all the commandments guarantees total forgiveness of sins and assures one of exaltation through that perfection which comes by complying with the formula the Lord gave us ... "Be ye therefore perfect, even as your Father which is in heaven is perfect" ... Perfection therefore is an achievable goal.[31]

It cannot be made any clearer than that. "Perfection is an achievable goal." It is also a necessary goal if one is to enjoy salvation. That's why Stephen Robinson's wife was beside herself (and so are many others). She could not live up to the standard teaching of Mormonism.

How beautifully, wonderfully, lavishly different the true Christian gospel is. It's true that sin leaves us in a pit. And it's true that repentance—a change of direction from going our own way to going God's way—is necessary in order for us to enter Christ's kingdom (Mark 1 v 15). But it's false to say that we need to (or that we can) climb out of the pit ourselves. It's false to say that our salvation depends on the thoroughness of our repentance or the strength of our will-power. It depends on God's grace. Paul—one of Christ's true apostles—wrote this:

> Because of his great love for us, God, who is rich in mercy, made us alive with Christ even when we were dead in transgressions—it is by grace you have been saved. And God raised us up with Christ and seated us with him in the heavenly realms in Christ Jesus, in order that in the coming ages he might show the incomparable riches of his grace, expressed in his kindness to us in Christ Jesus. For it is by grace you have been saved, through faith—and this is not from yourselves, it is the gift of God—not by works, so that no one can boast.
>
> **Ephesians 2 v 4-9**

Grace is not free in LDS theology. Grace is not grace. There is a precondition to attaining it. Having a "testimony" is only supposed to confirm the truth; it does not complete the job to be done, it only starts you off on your long climb up the ladder. Kimball says, "There is no promise nor indication of forgiveness to any soul who does not totally repent." If we are going to witness to Mormons effectively, we need to understand that the burden they bear is heavy. Jesus says in Matthew 11 v 28, "Come to me, all you who are weary and burdened, and I will give you rest."

Micah's story

Micah Wilder grew up in a strong Mormon home. He was taught that in and through his religious acts he could make himself right with God. As a teenager he moved to Utah where his mom became a professor at BYU, the flagship Mormon university.

Age 19, Micah left for a two-year mission trip to share the good news according to Mormonism, just like his two older brothers had. While on his mission in Florida, he was confident that he'd be able to convert many people. So confident, in fact, that he even went to a Baptist church and asked if he could share the gospel with the minister!

He sat with the minister and presented to him the Mormon gospel that there were ordinances and works to perform to get sins forgiven. The Baptist minister listened, and then told Micah that what he shared was not the true gospel of Jesus Christ according to the Bible. He spoke of the overwhelming love of God and his offer of free forgiveness, referencing Ephesians 2 v 8-9. Micah's initial response was to reject his message and argue back. But as Micah was leaving, the minister challenged him to go home and read the New Testament as if he were a child (Mark 10 v 15).

When Micah got back to his apartment, that's what he did for the first time in his life. He spent the rest of his two-year mission trip poring over the New Testament more than a dozen times. As he did so, he slowly came to see the grace of God in a way he never had before.

Three weeks before the end of Micah's trip, he was challenged by his LDS leaders about his changing faith. He testified that Jesus Christ alone was the way, the truth, and the life (John 14 v 6), and that the Mormon Church was not necessary for salvation. Micah was sent home in disgrace. The cost for embracing the true gospel was high, but Micah knew that he had a greater treasure in Christ.

Today, Micah is involved in evangelism to Mormons alongside other ex-Mormons (including his brother) through a ministry called Adam's Road Ministry.

Chapter five

Salvation, part 2: Making room for the gospel

We saw in the last chapter that Mormonism puts tremendous pressure on its members to perform. As a child, I resisted being baptized at the normal age of eight because I was so aware of the high standard set for living with Heavenly Father: perfection. I thought I'd beat the system by waiting to be baptized until my death bed. Surely this would ensure all my past sins were cleansed with little chance of messing things up! But, afraid of dying prematurely, I gave in pretty quickly and was baptized at age nine.

That said, not all Mormons would share the same concern as my 8-year-old self. Remember, there are two kinds of Mormon doctrine: folk Mormon doctrine (what people commonly believe) and Mormon Church doctrine (what the LDS Church officially teaches). The two are often very different when it comes to the topic of attaining eternal life.

If you ask a Mormon if they know that they have eternal life, they'll undoubtedly say yes. But they usually have in mind "immortality," living forever in the resurrection. This is a form of salvation which almost everyone gets, according to Mormonism. The Mormon Church defines "eternal life" as something different. The emphasis is on *quality*, not length. It is exaltation in celestial glory, living in the presence of Heavenly Father. The Doctrine and Covenants 14:7 says, "And if you keep my commandments and endure to the end you shall have eternal life, which gift is the greatest of all the gifts of God." To an LDS person, the greatest of all the gifts is more than just living forever. It is the good life, the best life; eternal life in celestial glory as an eternal family.

More knowledgeable Mormons will be aware of the requirement for attaining this "eternal life." The task is to eliminate all sin and obey all the commandments so that Christ's grace can be applied. But most Mormons are scarcely aware of the deadline. It is generally thought that it can be accomplished in the "spirit world," between death and resurrection. According to folk Mormonism, it is not only those who had no opportunity to hear the gospel in this life who have the opportunity to do so in the next one (as per Mormon Church teaching); instead, everyone gets another go. But neither this delay or the common maxim, "try, try your best and God will make up the rest" is official LDS doctrine. While "infinite perfection" won't be attained until the celestial kingdom, the LDS Church teaches that "finite perfection" can and must be reached in this life.

The conversation

So how do we go about engaging a Mormon friend on the subject of salvation?

First, we need to get clear precisely on what is required and then know the deadline by which that job must be accomplished; in other words, how and when moral perfection must be achieved in order for grace to be applied in accordance with Mormon theology. Remember, the likelihood is that your Mormon friend has served or is serving on a two-year mission. They are accustomed to being in the teaching position. Play on this by asking thought-provoking questions so as not to raise their defenses unnecessarily. The aim is to prompt reflection.

Pose the question to your Mormon friend or missionary: "Since I want nothing more than to know the truth of how I can spend eternity with Heavenly Father, please say *exactly* what would be required of me to enter into celestial glory." They will probably tell you that it requires something like faith, repentance, baptism, and the laying on of hands to receive the Holy Ghost.

Then ask them if they will kindly go through a series of troubling passages about salvation that someone showed you, or that you've located in your reading and research into the Book of Mormon and other teachings by Mormon authorities. If you can say (honestly) that you've personally read these passages that have troubled you, you won't risk conveying to them that you've been under the spell of "anti-Mormon" literature and are perceived to be attacking them. Make a list of the passages below, or mark them up in a copy of the Book of Mormon or bookmark them online, then you won't need to memorize them. The Mormon will appreciate your having taken the time to read them.

The aim in sharing these passages is for our friend to experience a new and urgent felt need often absent in Mormon thinking: a real need for the gospel, which means "good news." For all the Mormons out there like Janet (the stressed-out wife we read about in the previous chapter), there are others who don't really appreciate how high the bar is set (because they go by folk doctrine more than by Mormon Church doctrine).

The virtues of this conversational approach are several. It addresses an essential issue and gets to the heart of the matter, the gospel. It uses Mormon scriptures to create a felt need for grace. It speaks their religious language. And, finally, it allows us to appeal to the law as a "schoolmaster" to lead people to Christ. This is how Paul speaks of the law in Galatians 3 v 24 (King James Version). The law doesn't help us; it just leaves us helpless. It doesn't justify us; it just leaves us guilty before the judgment bar of a holy God. In other words, it shows us how much we need Jesus.

Key passages from Mormon scripture

You could start with Doctrine and Covenants 58:42-43:

> Behold, he who has repented of his sins, the same is forgiven, and I, the Lord, remember them no more. By this ye may know if a man repenteth of his sins— behold, he will confess them and forsake them.

Note carefully that to know with confidence that one's sins will be forgiven in order to get into heaven, one must repent of them. But here is the catch. To repent here means confessing each and every sin and then forsaking it. That is, stop committing sin.

Then consider the Pearl of Great Price, Articles of Faith, I.3:

> We believe that through the Atonement of Christ, all mankind may be saved, by obedience to the laws and ordinances of the Gospel.

Once again, Mormonism asserts that salvation is by grace (the atonement of Christ). But it is also—and this is significant—by obeying the laws and ordinances of the gospel. This begs the question, how many laws and ordinances? Think about how many laws and ordinances are laid out in the four-piece standard works (the Old and New Testaments; the Book of Mormon; Doctrine and Covenants; Pearl of Great Price). Point out to your friend how high the bar is.

This process of earning a right standing with God is summarized in the Book of Mormon: "for we know that it is by grace that we are saved, after all we can do" (2 Nephi 25:23). Elsewhere it says:

> Come unto Christ, and be perfected in him, and deny yourselves of *all* ungodliness; and if ye shall deny yourselves of *all* ungodliness, and love God with *all* your might, mind and strength, *then* is his grace sufficient for you, that by his grace ye may

be perfect in Christ ... And again, *if* ye by the grace of God are perfect in Christ, and deny not his power, *then* are ye sanctified in Christ by the grace of God, through the shedding of the blood of Christ, which is in the covenant of the Father unto *the remission of your sins,* that ye become holy, without spot. (Moroni 10:32-33, emphasis mine)

Some Mormons will be tempted to comment at this point that God does not really expect us to be perfect. He knows we will sin. I counsel Mormons to not lean on their own folk understanding but instead to submit to their own scriptures which say, "the Lord giveth *no* commandments unto the children of men, save he shall prepare a way for *them* that *they* may accomplish the thing which he commandeth them" (1 Nephi 3:7, emphasis mine).

Ask your friend, "Which command does God consider optional for obedience? Which is unimportant to God?" According to the Book of Mormon there is no command that God gives which cannot and should not be obeyed. Indeed, the quote above from Moroni 10 gives a clear conditional: getting the remission of sins, having them forgiven by grace, requires that the sinner *first* enter complete self-denial of all ungodliness and come to love God completely and wholeheartedly before the grace of the atonement can apply to one's life.

You could share the ladder illustration from the previous chapter: it is as though one must climb the entire ladder up the pit—be fully repentant and satisfactorily keep all the commandments all the time—in order to reach the prize, grace. This seems to nullify the very meaning of grace. Grace is not depicted here as a gift, but as something earned after a long, toilsome and near impossible mission.

So then, according to LDS scriptures, is salvation by grace? Yes! But there is an insurmountable obstacle of works that constitute the precondition to receiving it. This does not seem to be very good news. And the stakes are very high. Notice what happens to those who fail to endure (in other words, fail to stop sinning):

> And it shall come to pass, that whoso repenteth [stops sinning] and is baptized in my name shall be filled; and if he endureth to the end [does not go back to sinning], behold, him will I hold guiltless before my Father at that day when I shall stand to judge the world. And he that endureth not unto the end [does not stop sinning permanently, but returns to sinning], the same is he that is also hewn down and cast into the fire, from whence they can no more return, because of the justice of the Father ... And no unclean thing can enter into his kingdom; therefore nothing entereth into his rest save it be those who have washed their garments in my blood, because of their faith, and the repentance of *all* their sins, and their faithfulness unto the end ... Therefore, what manner of men ought ye to be? Verily I say unto you, even as I am. (3 Nephi 27:16, 17, 19, 27; emphasis mine)

Deadline for having one's sins forgiven

At this point in the conversation, many LDS people I talk with will claim that we have more time—that after we die there is still opportunity to repent and stop sinning. But this brings up the next important point about the LDS concept of salvation in folk vs official doctrine: namely, the deadline for achieving it.

The Book of Mormon is unmistakably clear about when the job must be completed. While some interpret the teaching of Spencer W. Kimball, which we read sections of in chapter 4, as pertinent only for matters of exaltation (that is, getting to the "best" section of heaven), the Book of Mormon on which he stands makes the deadline very clear. In Alma, we are told:

> For behold, this life is the time for men to prepare to meet God; yea, behold the day of this life is the day for men to perform their labors. And now, as I said unto you before, as ye have had so many witnesses, therefore, I beseech of you that ye do not procrastinate the day of your repentance until the end; for after this day of life, which is given us to prepare for eternity, behold, if we do not improve our time while in this life, then cometh the night of darkness wherein there can be no labor performed. Ye cannot say, when ye are brought to that awful crisis, that I will repent, that I will return to my God. Nay, ye cannot say this; for that same spirit which doth possess your bodies at the time that ye go out of this life, that same spirit will have power to possess your body in that eternal world. For behold,

if ye have procrastinated the day of your repentance even until death, behold, ye have become subjected to the spirit of the devil, and he doth seal you his; therefore, the Spirit of the Lord hath withdrawn from you, and hath no place in you, and the devil hath all power over you; and this is the final state of the wicked. (Alma 34:32-35)

The notion that there are many opportunities and many different kingdoms of heaven through which a Mormon might progress after this life is not found in the Book of Mormon. Can any sincere Mormon really think that the final state of the wicked, where the devil seals one as his and has all power over him, is any kind of heaven? This "eternal world" exists for people who have failed to adequately repent in this life. This explains why Kimball warns the faithful that any talk about "opportunities in the next life" is simply not an option for the Mormon person:

Christ became perfect through overcoming. Only as we overcome shall we become perfect and move toward godhood. As I have indicated previously, *the time to do this is now, in mortality* ... One cannot delay repentance until the next life, the spirit world, and there prepare properly for the day of judgment ... Men and women who live in mortality and who have heard the gospel here have had their day, their seventy years to put their lives in harmony, to perform the ordinances, to repent and to *perfect* their lives. (Emphasis mine)[32]

Lest someone be tempted to fall back on their childhood teaching of "try, try your best, and God will make up the rest," Kimball goes on to cut off that route. He uses the illustration of an army officer who gives instructions to an army private concerning a mission. After a series of inadequate replies from the private such as "I'll try," or "I'll do my best," all of which the officer rebukes, Kimball concludes the illustration by stating that the private is able-bodied and the task is reasonable to complete. He forcefully states that "trying is not sufficient."[33]

So far, I have provided more detail than you will probably need! Don't feel too overwhelmed. Just pick a couple of passages from Mormon scriptures that show the requirement and deadline for eternal life and use them to engage your Mormon friend. Then move on to the next step below—this last piece is critical.

The testimony of the gospel

In the official LDS view, salvation is by grace, through faith, after one has repented by eliminating sin to the point where all thought, urge, or desire to sin is completely gone. This is bad news, not good news. It is not the gospel that Jesus and the apostles preached. Further, this calls into question the Mormon "testimony," because Scripture is clear what God's "testimony" is concerning salvation. Draw your friend's attention to 1 John 5 v 9-13:

> We accept human testimony, but God's testimony is greater because it is the testimony of God, which he has given about his Son. Whoever believes in the Son of God accepts this testimony. Whoever

does not believe God has made him out to be a liar, because they have not believed the testimony God has given about his Son. And this is the testimony: God has given us eternal life, and this life is in his Son. Whoever has the Son has life; whoever does not have the Son of God does not have life. I write these things to you who believe in the name of the Son of God so that you may know that you have eternal life.

The "testimony" John is talking about is the testimony of God to us, through the Holy Spirit in us, regarding salvation. We know that this testimony is true, because God confirms it in Scripture. We can have assurance of our eternal destiny based on embracing what Jesus accomplished. Jesus is enough: "Whoever has the Son has life." It says we can "know" this. It uses the present tense in the Greek, that whoever has the Son has eternal life. Any testimony that rejects the doctrine that salvation is by grace alone, through faith alone, makes God a liar (since that is to assert that this passage is not true) and denies the testimony of the Holy Spirit. For any person who rejects this, he or she needs to question what spirit they are trusting.

For the Mormon, the plan of salvation involves a debt refinanced rather than a debt paid. But the biblical gospel with the biblical "testimony" involves God cancelling the debt through Christ, paying it in full. You could show your friend this passage:

When you were dead in your transgressions and the uncircumcision of your flesh, He made you alive

together with Him, having forgiven us all our transgressions, having canceled out the certificate of
debt consisting of decrees against us, which was
hostile to us; and He has taken it out of the way,
having nailed it to the cross.

Colossians 2 v 13-14, NASB

Here, the apostle Paul says that the gospel effectively "canceled out the certificate of debt." That's why Jesus' last words on the cross were "It is finished" (John 19 v 30).

There are only two kinds of people, and two kinds of religion: the "do" and the "done." The "do" people are still trying to perfect themselves. Perfection is the standard required by God, according to both the Book of Mormon and the Bible (Matthew 5 v 48). But the Bible substitutes Christ's perfect life for our own imperfect life.

In the movie *Saving Private Ryan*, Captain John Miller (played by Tom Hanks) sacrifices himself and many in his unit to save Private James Ryan (played by Matt Damon). Near the end of the movie, Captain Miller is dying from a fatal gunshot wound and says these last words to Private Ryan, "Earn this." For the rest of his life, Private Ryan carries the awful burden of trying to earn the sacrificial gift. At the end of the movie, Ryan, now transposed to the present time as an old man revisiting the gravesite of Captain Miller, asks his wife if he has been a good man. In desperation he turns toward the grave and tells Captain Miller that he hopes he has done enough.

For Bible believers, only Jesus lived the sinless life that is required, and we can count on his record as our own. Christians are "done" people, not "do" people. God does not lower his standard from complete righteousness. But rather than requiring that we become perfect on our own before the grace is applied (LDS route), we get the privilege of counting Christ's sacrificial atonement to our credit as though it were *our* righteousness. It is a gift not preconditioned on works, even though it inevitably leads to works.

The Book of Mormon claims that "we are saved by grace, after all we can do" (2 Nephi 25:23). The Bible says, "It is by grace you have been saved, through faith—and this is not from yourselves, it is the gift of God—not by works, so that no one can boast" (Ephesians 2 v 8-9). Salvation is by grace, through faith, as God's gift. Should we do works? Of course! Ephesians 2 v 10 says that there are good works which God has prepared in advance for us to do. But works are the fruit of salvation, not the root of salvation. God does not want us boasting. God, in Christ, is the hero of the salvation story.

Which brings us to our next major issue: the LDS concept of God.

Chapter six

God: Who do Mormons worship?

Do Mormons and Christians worship the same God? Short answer: no. For a longer answer, keep reading.

Christianity teaches that God is supreme and that he alone is worthy of worship. Is God infinite (without limits)? Is God all-powerful (omnipotent)? Is God all-loving (omnibenevolent)? Is God all-knowing (omniscient)? Is God eternal—without beginning or end? Is there only one God? The answer to all those questions is "yes" for the Christian. There is one God, who has characteristics that are unique to him, and who possesses power, knowledge, and goodness to the maximal degree. But the answer to all those questions is "no" for the Mormon, as indicated by two doctrines.

First, Mormons believe that there are many gods, who create and rule over other worlds. According to

LDS apostle Bruce McConkie, "[A] plurality of gods exist … there is an infinite number of holy personages, drawn from worlds without number."[34] Granted, there is only one God for our world according to LDS thinking; typically referred to as "Heavenly Father." So Mormons believe in many gods, but claim to worship only one God. Mormons may also speak of "God" in reference to "the Godhead," which in their view is a team of separate gods (rather than one God in three Persons).

Second, LDS authorities speak of the "law of eternal progression." Basically, this is the idea that it is possible to become a god or a goddess. Some Mormons will often defend this view before Christians, claiming that it is consistent with some of the early Christian church fathers. The apostle Peter, for instance, says that Christians "may participate in the divine nature" (2 Peter 1 v 4). But upon careful reflection, references like these do not at all mean what LDS people take them to mean. It is a matter of participating in the divine nature, not becoming divine by nature. Christians believe that we will, for all eternity—as humans—progress in our understanding and appreciation of the Lord as we worship and experience God. But this refers to an infinite God whose being is immeasurable, such that we can progress forever and never attain such divine greatness. We are, and will remain, human.

LDS Prophets and Godhood

Let's think some more about the problems and inconsistencies with the Mormon "law of eternal progression."

Some Christians don't believe that the LDS Church teaches this idea because some Mormons themselves deny it. I can still recall the astonishment I felt in 1997 when I first saw the cover article of August's *TIME Magazine*, where the Mormon prophet at that time, Gordon B. Hinckley, appeared to deny what was otherwise a main feature of Mormonism:

Interviewer [setting out the alleged LDS belief]: "God the Father was once a man as we were. This is something that Christian writers are always addressing. Is this the teaching of the [LDS] church today, that God the Father was once a man like we are?"

Hinckley: "I don't know that we teach it. I don't know that we emphasize it. I haven't heard it discussed for a long time in public discourse. I don't know. I don't know all the circumstances under which that statement was made. I understand the philosophical background behind it. But I don't know a lot about it and I don't know that others know a lot about it."[35]

Had Hinckley forgotten? Was he confused? Not likely. In fact, this seems to be a deliberate public-relations tactic when communicating with non-LDS people. Contrast that with what his own book, published two months before that interview, communicated to Mormons:

The whole design of the gospel is to lead us, onward and upward to greater achievement, even, eventually, to godhood. [This teaching was] enunciated by the prophet Joseph Smith in the King Follett Sermon (see *Teachings of the Prophet Joseph Smith*, pp. 342-62) and emphasized by President Lorenzo Snow. It is this grand and incomparable concept: As God now is, man may become![36]

The law of eternal progression isn't just the idea of some maverick teacher. It is rooted in Mormon scriptures themselves:

Then shall they be gods, because they have no end; therefore shall they be from everlasting to everlasting, because they continue; then shall they be above all, because all things are subject unto them. Then shall they be gods, because they have all power, and the angels are subject unto them. (Doctrine and Covenants 132:20)

In the words of Mormonism's founder Joseph Smith:

Here, then, is eternal life, to know the only wise and true God; and you have got to learn how to be Gods yourselves, and to be kings and priests to God, the same as all Gods have done before you, namely, by going from one small degree to another, and from a small capacity to a great one; from grace to grace, from exaltation to exaltation, until you attain to the resurrection of the dead and are able to dwell in everlasting burnings, and to sit in glory, as do those who sit enthroned in everlasting power.[37]

This doctrine has been upheld by numerous prophets and presidents in the centuries since, including Lorenzo Snow, referenced by Hinckley in the quote above. Snow recalled, "The Spirit of God fell upon me to marked extent and the Lord revealed to me, just as plainly as the sun at noon-day, this principle, which I put in a couplet: 'As man now is, God once was; As God now is, man may be.'"[38]

Snow did not see this "couplet" as anything less than divine revelation. So any proponent of Mormonism must either accept it as such, or claim that Snow did not hear from God. And if the latter, by what standard does such an LDS believer defend their own revelation or testimony from God, when they reject that of the one who is supposed to have had authority?

The trustworthiness of prophets and the "law of eternal progression"

Even among those Mormon authorities who promote the "law of eternal progression," there are an alarming number of inconsistencies. Again, we can use these inconsistencies to challenge our Mormon friends: if there really is a living prophet, shouldn't he at least be able to tell us about God?

Let's look at two opposing views: the "bound capacity" view and the "unbound capacity" view of eternal progression. The "bound capacity" view teaches that there is a sort of upper limit of divinity, as it were—such that it is possible to arrive at the status of being all-knowing, all-powerful and so on. The "unbound capacity" view emphasizes the perpetual divine progress—one just keeps getting more and more godlike forever.

Which of these does Mormonism affirm? Both and neither, depending on which Mormon is asked. The Book of Mormon does not engage in this sort of speculation, but the living prophets and apostles most certainly do. It seems that they are split and confused on the matter.

"Unbound capacity"
The second president and prophet, Brigham Young, chided those who limited the progress of all the gods by saying:

> According to [a different LDS apostle's] theory, God can progress no further in knowledge and power; but the God that I serve is progressing eternally, and so are his children: they will increase to all eternity, if they are faithful.[39]

For Christians, our eternal progression is always from depravity to ideal humanity; for Mormons, it is from humanity to divinity (and even with the step of perhaps becoming angels along the way). In this respect, humanity and divinity are not different in kind according to Mormonism (as we would distinguish between Creator and creature), but only in degree.

Writing some years after Young, the fourth president, Wilford Woodruff, wrote that "God is increasing in knowledge."[40] Following him, Lorenzo Snow taught that "We must advance through stages to godhood. As man now is, God once was—even the babe of Bethlehem, advancing to Childhood—thence to boyhood, manhood, then to the Godhead. This then is the 'mark of the prize of man's high calling in Christ Jesus.'"[41] According to this view, Jesus was a man who became a superman.

Yet if we stop to think about the "unbound capacity" interpretation of eternal progression, it throws up several problems. Suppose we believe that the gods progress in all characteristics of deity for eternity (rather than at some point arriving at omniscience, omnipotence, and so on). Then we can assume that the god who just began the transition into divinity is far behind the progress of the god that he was worshipping before he became a god himself. And that god that he worshipped is likewise far behind in progression compared to the god before him. In other words, if the process has been going on for all eternity, then the god that we worship in this world as God has a near infinite number of gods greater than he in knowledge, power, dominion, and so on. By comparison, he would seem to be a flea.

So why worship a "god" who is of the lowest rank amongst the infinite number of gods that must exist on that account? Is this not scraping from the bottom of the barrel in contrast to responding to a genuinely supreme being worthy of worship? In the "unbound capacity" view, God does not seem like a god at all, but a superman whose present powers you and me could potentially surpass one day. Of course, such a god will in turn be more powerful and knowledgeable by that time, as will his god, and his god's god, and so on. But the knowledge and power he has today can potentially be surpassed by you and me tomorrow.

"Bound capacity"

The second interpretation, bound capacity, has been supported by a number of different LDS prophets and apostles. The tenth president, Joseph Fielding Smith, taught that God does not progress eternally, but at some time will have arrived. His capacity is bound by some upper limit:

> It seems very strange to me that members of the Church will hold to the doctrine, 'God increases in knowledge as time goes on' ... Where has the Lord ever revealed to us that he is lacking in knowledge? That he is still learning new truth; discovering new laws that are unknown to him? I think this kind of doctrine is *very dangerous*.[42] (Emphasis mine, and also in the quotes that follow)

Don't miss that: view one ("unbound progression"), held by several prophets—not just Mormon Church members—is now considered dangerous.

One of the LDS apostles, Orson Pratt, remarked: "[the Gods] are all equal in knowledge, and in wisdom, and in the possession of all truth. None of these Gods are progressing in knowledge, neither can they progress in the acquirement of any truth." Further...

> Some have gone so far as to say that all the Gods were progressing in truth, and would continue to progress to all eternity, and that some were far in advance of others: but let us examine, for a moment, the *absurdity* of such a conjecture. If all the

Gods will be eternally progressing, then it follows, that there must be a boundless infinity of knowledge that no God ever has attained to, or ever can attain to, throughout infinite ages to come ... This is the great absurdity, resulting from the vague conjecture that there will be an endless progression in knowledge among all the Gods. Such a conjecture is not only *extremely absurd*, but it is in *direct opposition to what is revealed.*[43]

Thus, view one is not only dangerous but is also rationally absurd and contradicts revelation. Similarly, speaking in the 1980s, apostle Bruce R. McConkie indicated that many of the other General Authorities we quoted above were simply clueless:

There are those who say that God is progressing in knowledge and is learning new truths. *This is false—utterly, totally, and completely.* There is *not one sliver of truth in it.* It grows out of a *wholly twisted* and *incorrect* view of [Joseph Smith's] King Follett Sermon and of what is meant by eternal progression.[44]

These are harsh words—almost as harsh as Young's words that contradict them. The LDS Church's current position (which may, of course, change tomorrow) apparently affirms the "bound" view, but it is not entirely clear. What's more, ask five different Mormons and you will get six different opinions. The fact is that the LDS prophets themselves, who are supposed to know, really have no clue.

Each asserts his views confidently, even to the point of claiming that the other position is irrationally condemned and dangerous. Remember "the testimony" in a previous chapter? Can we really have a testimony that has faith in such living "prophets" who are irrational and dangerous? What is the point of having living prophets if they cannot agree on important and essential spiritual matters? Remember, these are not "secondary" issues, equivalent to ones upon which evangelicals might legitimately disagree; these are the fundamental questions about who God is.

If the Mormon you are speaking to affirms this second ("bound") interpretation of "eternal progression"—that is, that perfection in all God's attributes (omniscience, omnipotence, and so on) is arrived at over time—then we may inquire about the possibility of such a feat. How, for instance, is it even logically possible for a being to have acquired the last "bit" of knowledge so as to become infinitely knowledgeable (omniscient)? Just as I cannot reach infinity if I begin counting 1... 2... 3... 4... so I cannot ever reach the status of infinite knowledge by acquiring one bit at a time, no matter how many seconds or even centuries that might take. Progressing through successive addition will never bring about one's arrival. Asking your Mormon friend about these things will help them to see how great a leap of faith they are making.

The Bible describes God as the One "who has perfect knowledge" (Job 37 v 16) and "knows everything" (1 John 3 v 20), things actual and possible (Psalm 139 v 1-4); indeed, "his understanding is infinite" (Psalm 147 v 5, KJV). Beginning with a finite number, it is impossible to reach infinity by successive addition. The Mormon concept of "God" entails a being who began with a finite number of items known and reached infinite knowledge by successive addition. Therefore, this Mormon concept of God is impossible.

The "law of eternal progression" means that we are either faced with a Mormon God who is vastly inferior to other gods, who each possess far more power, knowledge, and so forth, than himself, and whose present qualities we can surpass in time while he is ever progressing to a great degree; or with a Mormon God whose nature seems to be incoherent and defy existence. Either way, these options do not square with biblical Christianity. The Mormon concept of God or gods is not the biblical one. And nor is the Mormon view of Jesus. That is the subject to which we'll turn next.

Chapter seven

Christ: The differences that matter

Many Christians think that Mormons are Christians because they speak of Christ, believe in Christ, and have Christ's name as part of their church name. But is this Jesus the biblical Jesus of historical Christianity? This is so important, because one can be wrong on every non-essential Christian doctrine and still go to heaven. But this is not the case on essential matters such as who Jesus is and how we are saved.

Many Mormons and non-Mormons have observed that the LDS Church seems to be talking about Jesus and his work more now than compared to the past. Is it just savvy public relations, in view of an ever-increasing dialogue between evangelicals and Mormons in North America? Whatever the reason, talking about Jesus more doesn't make you a Christian unless what you believe about him lines up with what the New Testament reveals. The "Mormon Jesus" and the Jesus whom Christians believe in are not the same. In this chapter we'll look at the main difference between them.

The Mormon Jesus

Robert Millet is likely the most prominent Mormon scholar writing today—at least in terms of public relations. Under the heading "What Mormons Believe About Jesus Christ," located on the official LDS resource for news media and the public, is an address he gave at Harvard Divinity School.[45]

Here, Millet outlines several familiar beliefs that Mormons hold about Jesus, in common with Christians. For example, that he is the Messiah and the Son of God; and the fact of his incarnation, death, resurrection, and exaltation to heaven. Elsewhere, Millet claims that Jesus was not only the Son of God, but God the Son, and that he exists from eternity past to eternity future: "He was also God and is certainly God today." Millet even refers to Jesus as "the self-existing One."[46] So there seems to be a great deal of initial harmony with the historical Christian view of Jesus' divinity. The subtitle to the Book of Mormon, added in 1982, is "Another Testament of Jesus Christ." Millet claims that in the Book of Mormon, "Christ or his ministry is mentioned approximately every 1.7 verses."[47]

Highlighting and repeating the word "Jesus" may make him central to LDS consciousness, but it is still a far cry from connecting to who Jesus really is. There remains a fundamental lack of correspondence to the real Jesus of Christian theology, history, philosophy, and Scripture. We might use the same words, but those words have different meanings.

While some Mormon voices like Millet promote the similarities, other LDS prophetic authorities, such as Gordon B. Hinckley, note the differences: "The traditional Christ of whom they speak is not the Christ of whom I speak."[48]

The problem is that the Mormon view of God (and man) directly impacts their view of Christ. As we saw in the previous chapter, in his King Follett Sermon Joseph Smith taught that God was once a man who lived on an earth and was later exalted, the same as all gods have been in the past.[49] While polytheism and the progression toward godhood is not found in the Book of Mormon, it was certainly part of Smith's theology and is grounded in other Mormon scriptures (for example, the Book of Abraham in the Pearl of Great Price and the Doctrine and Covenants section 132). Jesus is only one of an infinite number of finite gods in Mormonism.

When it comes to the identity of Christ, the problem isn't their failure to embrace Jesus' humanity per se or his divinity per se. Indeed, Mormons embrace the humanity and divinity of Jesus just as they do of all persons—including you and I. They conflate these natures and think of them as being on one continuum. So the problem is that Jesus is in no way unique.

For instance, a Mormon can claim that both God and man are eternal. According to *The Encyclopedia of Mormonism*, Joseph Smith said that "the spirit of man is not a created being; it existed from eternity" and that when God "creates" something that merely means "to organize."[50] All beings, it is believed, including Jesus, have existed for all eternity as some sort of spirit matter. All beings exist on a scale of divinity, moving upwards.

The Christian view of humanity and divinity is very different: humans are created, while only God has existed forever. This means that the Christian view of Jesus is very different from Mormonism too: he is one person, with two distinct natures—human and divine. Mormons confuse and merge the natures (not just in Jesus, but in all of us). Understanding the precise relation of these two distinct natures in one person was what the major church Council of Chalcedon (AD 451) was all about. The council issued a definition that has set the boundaries for Christian theology in this area in the West ever since:

> Our Lord Jesus Christ is ... truly God and truly Man; ... One and the Same Christ, Son, Lord, Only-begotten; acknowledged in Two Natures unconfusedly, unchangeably, indivisibly, inseparably.

One person, two natures. The biblical evidence clearly points to Jesus Christ being fully man and fully God, yet those two natures exist in only one person, unconfused. How can this be? Christian thinkers throughout the centuries have found this mystery to be ultimately incomprehensible, yet entirely coherent. Yet to the Mormon there is no mystery in the fact that Jesus is fully God and fully man, because God is man and man is God on a single spectrum in LDS thought.

Supreme being or superman? A question about worship-worthiness

So, if the real Jesus is fully God—the supreme being—then he is worthy of worship. As we saw in the previous chapter, in Christian theology God is omnipotent (all-powerful), omniscient (all-knowing), and omnibenevolent (wholly good). "Great is our Lord and mighty in power; his understanding has no limit," declares the psalmist (Psalm 147 v 5). And so too is our risen Lord Jesus: "At the name of Jesus every name should bow, in heaven and on earth and under the earth, and every tongue acknowledge that Jesus Christ is Lord, to the glory of God the Father" (Philippians 2 v 10-11). By contrast, the finite "Superman Jesus" of Mormonism is not worship-worthy—he's just a human a few steps ahead of us.

Another prominent characteristic of God and therefore of Christ (mentioned in word but lacking in meaning by Millet, and Mormons more generally) is God's aseity (from the Latin, *a se*, meaning by itself or in itself). God exists *a se*—in other words, God is self-existent. He is self-sufficient; he doesn't rely on any other being; he is the uncreated Creator of all things (Isaiah 40 v 17-23, 28). Mormonism doesn't even have a Creator; rather, it has an organizer. Such a being is merely co-eternal with other matter in existence (D&C 131:7-8, Book of Abraham in the Pearl of Great Price 3:18-28).

By contrast, the Bible declares that all things exist by God's will (Revelation 4 v 11). The Gospel-writer John reconnects to the first words of Genesis in the origin of all things by the expression "In the beginning..." (John

1 v 1-3). He says that "the Word" was with God, was God, and that all things were made through him—in other words, all things came to be other than the Creator, who has always been. The Word became flesh in Jesus (v 14).

Later in the New Testament Paul says of God that "from him and through him and for him are all things" (Romans 11 v 36). In other words, God is the source, sustainer, and the goal of all reality outside himself. God didn't come into being, or progress from a finite being to an infinite one (a logical impossibility). He simply exists, as God, "from everlasting to everlasting" (Psalm 90 v 2). So too, we're told that Christ is the "exact representation of [God's] being," and that everything visible or invisible was created by him, and by him all things hold together (Hebrews 1 v 1-3; Colossians 1 v 15-17; see also 1 Corinthians 8 v 5-6; Philippians 2 v 5-8).

All this is what Christians mean when we say that Jesus is the Son of God, or God the Son. These are terms that Mormons claim to embrace, but deny in meaning. This is a common experience for which we need to be prepared when engaging with Mormons. They use the same terms. But these mean radically different things. Mormons do not make the radical distinction between humanity and divinity that Western theists do in Judaism, Christianity, and Islam. The Mormon gods have more in common with the page you are reading (that is, finite) than with the Western concepts of God (infinite!). So while there are apparent similarities between the Christian and Mormon ideas of Jesus, the differences are fundamental.

Conversation by illustration

So how do we take all this and turn it into a helpful gospel conversation with a Mormon friend or missionary?

In talking about Christ with Mormons, it is important to focus on the differences that make the difference. But this assumes that both parties accept that there *are* differences between Christianity and Mormonism. Many Mormons initially soft-peddle differences until forced to admit them. So I try to engage with them by illustration.

Me: "Let me ask you a personal question. Do you have a mom?"

Mormon: [Smiling, will reply] "Yes, of course."

Me: "I do too! Can you spell that?"

Mormon: "Umm... M.O.M."

Me: "No way. I spell it the same way. Maybe we have the same mom?" I ask, "Can you spell it backwards?"

Mormon: "M.O.M."

Me: [Excitedly, I blurt out] "Surely, we have the same mom because it is spelled the same!"

Upon further describing our respective moms, if hers is 6 feet tall and mine only 4 feet tall, then they are two different moms. One can then point out that while we all spell "Christ" and "God" the same way, the meanings aren't necessarily the same. This silly series of questions illustrates the point with light-hearted humor—just be careful to keep the tone fun and playful, not patronizing or condescending!

Mormons often claim to be Christians because they believe in Christ (and many Christians agree): hence, the need to define terms in our conversations. Do this by asking questions. This opens reflective dialogue, demonstrates genuine interest, and allows one to understand what the Mormon really believes, not merely what we think they believe. It also helps our Mormon friend to clarify and "own" their beliefs.

Good questions to ask are:

- Is Christ the Son of God?
- Is he God the Son?
- What do you mean by God?
- Is Christ God?
- Has Christ always been God?
- Is God supreme?
- How can God be supreme unless he's always been supreme? On your view, wouldn't Christ be steps behind his own Heavenly Father and other gods who are likewise eternally progressing for all eternity, thus preventing him from ever being supreme?

Mormons often give an affirmative response to most of those questions, but asking from different angles probes the depth of the issue so that one will inevitably arrive at a difference between the two of you—and that reveals Mormonism's entirely different view of reality.

As we've seen, Mormonism isn't really "another testimony of Jesus Christ" as the Book of Mormon subtitle supposes, but rather a testimony of another Jesus Christ. Our love for Christ and love for Mormons compels us to compassionately and truthfully approach them with the true gospel. Mormons are sincere about their faith. One can be sincere and wrong on every minor doctrine of the faith and still be saved. But if one is wrong on the essentials, one can lose one's soul. Mormonism teaches a different God in the name of a different Jesus and offers a different gospel than biblical Christianity. For this reason, we must love the Mormon enough to share with him or her the truth.

Barbara's story

Although Barbara Hoggan was raised as a Protestant, she always loved learning about other people's faiths and visiting churches that were different. Eventually she went on to join one of the churches that she visited; one that claimed 12 current apostles and a living prophet who walks and talks with the Almighty. In other words, a Mormon church. Because of that, she married a Mormon and raised her children in the LDS faith. She and her husband served for 25 years in their local Mormon ward.

But soon after she retired, Barbara started to question the LDS Church's teaching. She began to see that her Savior was all she needed. She and her husband endured a successful struggle to leave Mormonism, knowing that God's grace was eternal and infinite, much more than what they'd envisioned for so long.

But without a church to belong to, Barbara found that she missed it. She missed God being the focus of the Sabbath, of praising and worshipping him in prayer and in song. She missed learning about him. She missed living her life for him. So she found a Bible-believing church to belong to, and on Palm Sunday, she publicly accepted Christ as her Savior and was baptized.

She describes those early days of her new-found faith as like being at a banquet, gorging on God's word, having been starved for years. She couldn't get enough! But she had a thousand questions. Today, Barbara's found that, although she'll never know all the answers, she can rest in God's grace. She's happier than she's ever been because God is revealing himself to her through his word, day by day and week by week.

Chapter eight
Practical ways to engage

We started this book by comparing two unhelpful approaches to engaging with Mormons: the "bash" and "dash" approach. The "dash" approach is to open the door quickly and simply say, "I have a religion. Thanks, but no thanks. Bye!" But having read this far, you're probably now at greater risk of the "bash" approach—trying to prove Mormons wrong by throwing an overwhelming number of Bible verses at them!

While this book has explored doctrinal differences and dialogue, when engaging with Mormons—whether they're missionaries or friends you know socially—it's important to add a personal touch. All our endeavors with Mormons must start from a place of love: love for the Lord Jesus, and love for our Mormon neighbors. The aim is to build a real friendship and a bridge to sharing the gospel. These are people for whom Christ died and we should winsomely seek to share the good news with them as if it matters—because it does.

Are we willing to do for the truth what Mormons are doing for a lie?

Engaging with missionaries at your door and in your home

The LDS Church sends out 70,000 young missionaries to the field every year, resulting in around a quarter of a million converts. These young people sacrifice 18-24 months (depending on whether one is female or male), with phone contact with their family kept at a minimum (although there are more opportunities to email). One friend of mine, now an embittered atheist, remembers how even when his dad was dying, he was encouraged to remain on his mission rather than return home to see him. He resents the LDS Church today because he couldn't even be at his father's funeral.

The trips are largely self-funded. Since missionaries are on a tight budget, an invitation to dinner is always likely to be warmly received. Many Christians reject them, so this will set you apart and give you a platform to share Christ. That is not to say that we are now supporting their cause! We are simply extending hospitality—an essential Christian virtue.

While LDS missionaries are often guarded and generally don't want to give a hint of possible doubt, this is a time when many do begin to form doubts. One reason they have a companion (usually, they come in two's) is not only so that the older can mentor the young but also for accountability. This means they will be reluctant to admit their doubts in front of their partner. Even so, seeing Christ in true believers, especially if the missionary comes from a predominantly Mormon place like Utah, can be a life-changing experience.

Before setting out on their missionary experience, they go through a ceremony at the LDS temple, begin wearing special underwear called "temple garments," and have what we might call "basic training" at an MTC (Missionary Training Center). Here, they have the rudiments of the faith reinforced and memorize a conversational presentation. They are then assigned, as a matter of "calling," a certain location to serve their mission. Their day-to-day activity is predominantly door-knocking. This will probably be the most obvious opportunity for Christians to invite them into our homes.

If you have a Mormon friend from another area of your life with whom you spark up a spiritual conversation, it will almost inevitably lead to them asking if they can meet with you in your home or their home with the LDS missionaries assigned to your area. This is true even if your friend formerly served an LDS mission themselves. You'll need to decide if you want to say yes or would rather simply meet with your friend and keep that conversation going between the two of you.

The five missionary discussions
When sharing their faith with non-Mormons, missionaries are trained to cover the following material over the course of five meetings with the enquirer. More details can be found on the LDS Church website.

1. **The restoration of the gospel:** This sets up the rest of the discussions. It contends that after the time of

Christ's first apostles in the first century, there was a "Great Apostasy" or falling away and an essential loss of the priestly authority to act for God, until the restoration by God through Joseph Smith. This discussion is intended to highlight the need for a living prophet with proper priesthood.

2. **The plan of salvation:** This focuses on God's relationship to humanity, including the distinctive Mormon teaching that we were all together in the pre-existence. But if we pass the test on earth we can all return to live with Heavenly Father one day.

3. **The gospel of Jesus Christ:** The missionaries will move quickly to encourage the investigator (that's you!) to baptism. This lesson focuses on the necessity of baptism by proper priestly authority in the progress to merit eternal life.

4. **The commandments:** Here the investigator is informed of the need to keep the commands, and they are also given insight into what some of those commands are, including special dietary restrictions (like avoiding coffee), which must be observed if one is to enter into celestial glory. One is introduced to tithing, temple rituals, and the need for faithfulness and obedience to God's leaders on earth. (To the savvy Bible-loving Christian, this might feel reminiscent of the 613 commandments found in the Old Testament Torah!)

5. **Laws and ordinances:** One of the Articles of Faith in Mormonism teaches that we are saved by maintaining the laws and ordinances of the gospel. These include

post-baptism activities like priesthood ordination, temple work for the dead, and temple marriage.

I encourage strong Christians to invite missionaries into their homes and willingly take part in these discussions, because it takes the missionaries off the streets and limits them from converting others, opens up gospel opportunities, and helps Christians learn how to better articulate why they believe what they believe.

When taking part in the discussions, you are free to stay in "learner mode" during all five sessions—mainly just listening—in order to understand the whole of their presentation. If the missionaries try to get commitments or conversation out of you, simply express that you're enjoying learning and will share more after you've heard their whole presentation. This gives you time to reflect and prepare your response. In addition, when you do respond, you'll have earned the "right" to be heard in return.

Alternatively, you can enter into dialogue along the way. For example, during the discussion about God and humans, you could refer to the questions raised in chapter 6. During a salvation discussion, use the pointers from chapter 5.

Most importantly, over the five weeks pray that God opens the missionary's eyes and gives you insight and words to speak. Come across as a truth-seeker and as someone who loves them personally, as is appropriate of any true follower of Christ. When the time comes for you to share more fully, deploy some of the approaches from previous chapters, or ask them to read through

Romans or Galatians with you. Encourage them to read the New Testament as a child would and share your testimony with them passionately, as this is the language they understand.

Good L.I.S.T.E.Ning

Listening is good advice for any evangelistic encounter, but especially so with Mormons. I recommend an approach by my friend, David Geisler. He uses an acrostic LISTEN.

- **Learn their story:** Ask them personal questions during the five-week encounter (for example, Why is your faith so important to you? What is it about your faith that attracts you? If there were any areas of frustration about your faith, or areas where you wished you knew more, what might they be?). If we listen, we might glean what the individual Mormon actually believes and feels, rather than what we think they are supposed to believe or feel. Learn what their personal motives, reasons, or problems are so that you can better address the individual more than just the religion.
- **Invest time in them:** While there may be opportunities to socialize outside of the discussions, you can certainly build in time at the beginning or end of the discussions for that. Ask questions that remove yourself from the formal "project" of them trying to teach you. This could be over dinner or punch and cookies (but not coffee!).
- **Search for gaps:** As we're listening and paying attention to their words, attitudes, and responses, look

for gaps in their beliefs (contradictions, incoherencies, and so on). Keep a mental note of what these are and write them down after your meetings so that you don't forget. Then at the right time, perhaps after the five discussions are completed, you can select which is best to address. This is not only effective in itself, but has the additional benefit of showing that you were paying attention to them, earning you more credibility and a right to speak.

- **Throw light on the conversation:** There's always a danger that our attempts to engage with Mormons will generate more heat than light! But unless we want our first conversation with the Mormon to be the last, it is wise to not simply dump a laundry list of positions that are contradictory to Christian belief. We're not trying to win by using overwhelming fire power. Instead, attempt to generate more light than heat by asking questions and making observations. Early on, ask clarifying type questions on important doctrines, such as "What do you mean by...?" Or "Can you explain...?"

- **Expose the gaps:** This is where you can raise thought-provoking questions. Questions help minimize defensiveness and encourage reflection. In a gentle way, help them to see some of the inconsistencies that make it difficult for you to "come on board." Remember that Mormons dislike contention. But one can contend for the faith without coming across as being contentious.

- **Navigate in the conversation:** Aim to be in control of the conversation by the questions you ask.

The questions are meant to lead somewhere. After the initial clarifying questions, used targeted questions focused on essential doctrines concerning salvation, Christ, and God, which we covered in depth in the last few chapters. We want to ask questions that raise doubt, clarify, and create a desire to go further. While it may seem otherwise, you are actually on the offensive in an inoffensive way. In this way, you're still allowing the missionary to "teach," while you're the one teaching (indirectly) as you navigate the conversation.

Invitations to church

Many Mormons (including missionaries) will accept a simple invitation to attend your church. It is almost guaranteed that they will invite you to their Mormon church. So, fair is fair—invite them to yours! Granted, there are some churches which may be off-putting to Mormons, humanly speaking, especially if the worship feels performance-oriented or the teaching is weak. But, assuming that your church is a welcoming, Jesus-loving, Bible-teaching community, inviting a Mormon along could be very positive.

Remember, Mormonism is an experience-based religion. So let them experience a worship service with authentic believers and good teaching. When I became a Christian this was, for me, the other side of the coin to hearing the gospel—as I was enveloped into a Christlike community, I saw in life what the gospel message said in words. The community of people who had been redeemed and transformed by God's grace was attractive.

The average Mormon does not see passionate worship at their church. It is deeply religious, to be sure; but the awed and heart-felt worship on display at many Christian churches will feel noticeably different. Leaving something enthusiastic in the memory of a Mormon can be a good thing. A baby dedication or baptism service is also a great opportunity to invite a Mormon to church, since Mormons love families.

Social invitations

Mormonism, remember, attracts people with its sense of community. Furthermore, if a Mormon were to leave the LDS Church that might mean losing their whole sense of community, so they need to see that the Christian church could provide an alternative community.

So invite your Mormon friend to a church social event, your small group, or your house. If your Mormon friend is reluctant to come to a Sunday service, there are multiple different events that Christian communities hold that could be more neutral and inviting as a first step— perhaps a BBQ or an ice cream social.

And if there is nothing like that on your church schedule, organize your own! Introduce them to your Christian friends. Or it could be as simple as baking your Mormon friend some cookies and taking them round. Get to know them. Ask them personal (but socially appropriate!) questions. Show genuine appreciation for the "good" things in Mormon culture. It does wonders for building bridges rather than walls. It heightens their curiosity as to why you aren't LDS if there is so much you can appreciate about it. Love your Mormon friend and share the truth.

Love wills the good of the other. Mormons need to hear the true gospel about the true Jesus and one true God. But they also need to see it lived out in a community. Let's love God by loving Mormons for whom Christ died.

Corey's story

I grew up in Utah as a seventh-generation Mormon. One of my ancestors was even a personal bodyguard of Joseph Smith!

As a child, I earnestly led an active Mormon life, despite growing up in a broken home. As a young teen I became disenchanted with the hypocrisy I discovered in the Mormon community. But I didn't initially reject the God of Mormonism I loved.

When I was 16 I was invited to spend the summer in California with a Christian friend and his family. While there, we both spent a week at a Christian church camp. Although I was less active in Mormonism by this time, I had absolutely no intention of joining another religion. But on the camp I found myself drawn to Christ. The speaker presented the gospel in a way that was different than anything I'd ever heard before. My view of Jesus was radically altered as I came to understand grace for the first time. Although I had fears about leaving the religion I'd inherited, those were minimized by the security I found in Christ and the love I received from the Christians I met. I had never encountered anything like them— their worship was real and love authentic.

I ended up spending a year in California, being discipled, and then returned to Utah for a final year before high school graduation. The pressure was on to return to Mormonism. Somewhat confused and experiencing doubt about my decision to leave Mormonism, I read through the Book of Mormon again, but found it hollow and problematic.

I still had questions about the Bible and God's existence, until a friend introduced me to some Christian apologetics material. As I explored the evidence in support of biblical Christianity, it confirmed my confidence in the life-changing encounter I'd had with Jesus.

I have been passionate about evangelism ever since. Today, I am a philosophy professor and President of the national university campus ministry, Ratio Christi, a movement on 125 campuses dedicated to equipping students and faculty with reasons to follow Jesus.

Resources

Books for further reading

- Johnson, Eric and Sean McDowell, *Sharing the Good News with Mormons: Practical Strategies for Getting the Conversation Started* (Eugene, OR: Harvest House, 2018).
- Kerns, Travis S. *The Saints of Zion: An Introduction to Mormon Theology* (Nashville, TN: B&H Academic 2018).
- McKeever, Bill and Eric Johnson, *Mormonism 101: Examining the Religion of the Latter-day Saints* (Grand Rapids: Baker, 2015).
- Miller, Corey and Lynn K. Wilder, *Leaving Mormonism: Why Four Scholars Changed Their Minds* (Grand Rapids: Kregel, 2019).
- Rowe, David L. *I Love Mormons: A New Way to Share Christ with Latter-day Saints* (Grand Rapids: Baker, 2014).
- Wilder, Lynn K. *Unveiling Grace: The Story of How We Found Our Way Out of the Mormon Church* (Grand Rapids: Zondervan, 2013).

Websites

- Adams Road: www.adamsroadministry.com/ministering-to-mormons
- Mormon Info: www.Mormoninfo.org
- Mormonism Research Ministry: www.mrm.org
- Utah Lighthouse Ministry: www.utlm.org

Endnotes

1   https://www.cnn.com/2018/08/17/us/mormon-church-name-trnd/index.html.

2   https://www.mormonnewsroom.org/style-guide.

3   The Mormon Church is concerned with northern hemisphere shrinking but excited about the growth in the southern hemisphere. The geopolitical and religious heart of Mormonism is Utah. Salt Lake County is now only 49% Mormon, Utah County where Brigham Young University exists is 82%, and the state of Utah itself is only 62% Mormon. Abroad, however, it is experiencing a large growth rate with 3.5 million members in Brazil, Mexico, and the Philippines. Jana Riess, "Mormon growth continues to slow, especially in the US," https://religionnews.com/2018/04/13/mormon-growth-continues-to-slow-especially-in-the-u-s/ (accessed February 21, 2019). See also David Stewart, *The Cumorah Project*, http://www.cumorah.com/index.php (accessed February 21, 2019). Further, https://www.arkansasonline.com/news/2018/dec/16/mormons-on-decline-in-utah-20181216/?news-national.

4   Tad Walch, "At BYU, Baptist Says Mormons and Evangelicals 'May Go to Jail Together,'" Deseret News, October 21, 2013, http://www.deseretnews.com/article/865588850/At-BYU-Baptist-says-Mormons-and-evangelicals-may-go-to-jail-together.html?pg=all (accessed July 23, 2020).

5   Ross Anderson, *Understanding Your Mormon Neighbor:*

A Quick Christian Guide for Relating to Latter-day Saints (Zondervan, 2011), 20.

6   Rodney Stark, "Modernization and Mormon Growth: The Secularization Thesis Revisited," in *Contemporary Mormonism: Social Science Perspectives*, ed. Marie Cornwall, Tim B. Heaton, and Lawrence A. Young (University of Illinois Press, 1994), 14

7   Joseph Smith, *History of the Church*, 7 vols., ed. B. H. Roberts, 2nd ed. (Deseret Book, 1978), 1:19.

8   Joseph Smith, *History of the Church*, 1:40-41.

9   Bruce R. McConkie, *Mormon Doctrine* (Bookcraft, 1966), 670.

10 Joseph Smith, *Doctrines of Salvation: Sermons and Writings of Joseph Fielding Smith*, 3 vols., ed. and comp. Bruce R. McConkie (Bookcraft, 1955), 1:190.

11 Roberts, *History of the Church*, 6:408-09.

12 Bruce R. McConkie, *Mormon Doctrine*, 2nd ed (Deseret, 1979), 318.

13 James Faulconer, "Why a Mormon Won't Drink coffee but Might Have a Coke: The Atheological Character of the Church of Jesus Christ of Latter-day Saints," lecture, Brigham Young University, Provo, UT, March 19, 2003. Cited in Travis Kerns, *The Saints of Zion*, 20.

14 Boyd K. Packer, *That All May Be Edified* (Bookcraft, 1982), 340. Given the pervasive influence of testimony in Mormonism, it is surprising that the way to discover it is simply by repeating it.

15 Boyd K. Packer, "The Candle of the Lord," Ensign (January 1983): 55.

16 Dallin Oaks, "Teaching and Learning by the Spirit," Ensign (March 1997): 13.

17 Gene R. Cook, "Are You a Member Missionary?" *Ensign* (Conference Edition) (May 1976), 103.

18 Church of Jesus Christ of Latter-day Saints, *Preach My Gospel: A Guide to Missionary Service* (Intellectual Reserve, 2004), 38.

19 The expression "eternal life" represents "Celestial Glory," the highest heaven, for Mormons.

20 Stephen E. Robinson, *Are Mormons Christians?* (Deseret Book, 1998), 104-105.

21 Stephen E. Robinson, *Are Mormons Christians?*, 108.

22 Spencer W. Kimball, *The Miracle of Forgiveness* (Bookcraft, 1969), 206.

23 Boyd K. Packer, *Ensign* (May 1977), 54-55.

24 *Gospel Principles* (The Church of Jesus Christ of Latter-day Saints, 2009), 63-65.

25 *The Miracle of Forgiveness*, 200.

26 Stephen Robinson, *Believing Christ: The Parable of the Bicycle and Other Good News* (Deseret Book, 1992), 15-16. The other quotes in this chapter can also be found here.

27 While one cannot draw a definitive causal link between Utah's phenomenal depression and stress levels relative to religious beliefs, since correlation is not identical to causation, there is strong correlation between beliefs and behavior. Not only does such an extreme performance mentality generate a high degree of stress, but it also creates greater likelihood that people will be driven to hide their sin more than usual. LDS missionaries are often pointing to the fruits of Mormonism to confirm their message. Utah is also known for its secret sins like being the porn

consumer capital of the country. Elaine Jarvik, "Utah No. 1 in Online Porn Subscriptions, Report Says," Deseret News, March 3, 2009, https://www.deseret.com/2009/3/3/20304992/utah-no-1-in-online-porn-subscriptions-report-says (accessed September 17, 2019).

28 Kimball, *The Miracle of Forgiveness,* 203; italics mine.

29 Kimball, *The Miracle of Forgiveness,* 354–355; italics mine.

30 Kimball, *The Miracle of Forgiveness,* 170.

31 Kimball, *The Miracle of Forgiveness,* 208-9. It should be noted that when Mormons speak of "eternal life" in the ultimate sense they mean exaltation or "Celestial Glory."

32 Kimball, *The Miracle of Forgiveness,* 209-210, 213-214.

33 Kimball, *The Miracle of Forgiveness,* 164.

34 Bruce R. McConkie, *Mormon Doctrine* (Second Edition), 576-77.

35 Richard Ostling, *TIME Magazine* (August 4, 1997). To see discussion and correspondence on the LDS response concerning the authenticity of the reporting by TIME see: http://mit.irr.org/dodging-and-dissembling-prophet.

36 Gordon B. Hinckley, *Teachings of Gordon B. Hinckley* (Deseret Book, June 1997), 179.

37 *Teachings of the Prophet Joseph Smith, Selected by Joseph Fielding Smith* (Deseret Book, 1976), 346-347.

38 Lorenzo Snow, *The Teachings of Lorenzo Snow*, ed. Clyde Williams (Bookcraft, 1984), 2. On the same page Snow maintains that gods will be "increasing eternally."

39 Brigham Young, January 13, 1867, *Journal of Discourses,* 11:286.

40 Wilford Woodruff, *The Discourses of Wilford Woodruff* (Bookcraft, 1990), 3.

41 Snow, *The Teachings of Lorenzo Snow*, 5.

42 Joseph Fielding Smith, *Doctrines of Salvation* (Bookcraft 1954-56), Vol 1:7-8.

43 Orson Pratt, *The Seer*, 117, as cited in *In Their Own Words: A Collection of Mormon Quotations*, comp. Bill McKeever (Morris Publishing), 104

44 Bruce R. McConkie, "The Seven Deadly Heresies," an address given at BYU on June 1, 1980. Transcribed from actual speech, but emphasis mine.

45 https://www.mormonnewsroom.org/article/what-mormons-believe-about-jesus-christ.

46 Robert L. Millet and Gerald R. McDermott, *Claiming Christ: A Mormon-Evangelical Debate* (Brazos Press, 2007), 46-48, 50.

47 Millet and McDermott, *Claiming Christ*, 61.

48 https://www.thechurchnews.com/archives/1998-06-20/crown-of-gospel-is-upon-our-heads-127227 (accessed July 23, 2020).

49 Joseph Fielding Smith, comp., *Teachings of the Prophet Joseph Smith* (Deseret Book, 1976), 342-62.

50 Daniel H. Ludlow (ed), *The Encyclopedia of Mormonism*, Vol 2:867-8 (Macmillan, 1992), 867-868.

Reach out with the gospel

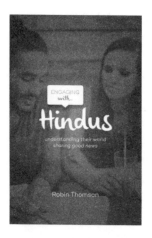

Engaging with Hindus
by Robin Thomson

Robin Thomson spent 20 years in India teaching the Bible and training church leaders. He is the author of several books relating the Bible to Asian culture.

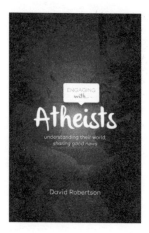

Engaging with Atheists
by David Robertson

David Robertson is the director of Third Space, a project of the City Bible Forum in Australia, having formerly been minister of St Peter's Free Church in Dundee, Scotland. He is the author of *The Dawkins Letters*, and has publicly debated Richard Dawkins and other prominent atheists throughout the UK and Europe.

www.thegoodbook.com | .co.uk | .com.au | .co.nz   **thegoodbook** COMPANY

in a multi-cultural society

Engaging with Muslims
by John Klaassen

John Klaassen is Associate Professor of Global Studies at Boyce College, in Louisville Kentucky, USA. Previously he worked in relief and development in North Africa.

Engaging with Jewish People
by Randy Newman

Randy Newman has worked with Campus Crusade for more than twenty years, teaching seminars at a variety of locations from college campuses to the Pentagon.

www.thegoodbook.com | .co.uk | .com.au | .co.nz

BIBLICAL | RELEVANT | ACCESSIBLE

At The Good Book Company, we are dedicated to helping Christians and local churches grow. We believe that God's growth process always starts with hearing clearly what he has said to us through his timeless word—the Bible.

Ever since we opened our doors in 1991, we have been striving to produce Bible-based resources that bring glory to God. We have grown to become an international provider of user-friendly resources to the Christian community, with believers of all backgrounds and denominations using our books, Bible studies, devotionals, evangelistic resources, and DVD-based courses.

We want to equip ordinary Christians to live for Christ day by day, and churches to grow in their knowledge of God, their love for one another, and the effectiveness of their outreach.

Call us for a discussion of your needs or visit one of our local websites for more information on the resources and services we provide.

Your friends at The Good Book Company

thegoodbook.com | thegoodbook.co.uk
thegoodbook.com.au | thegoodbook.co.nz
thegoodbook.co.in